STORYBOOK BIRTHDAY PARTIES

Cindy Dingwall

Alleyside Press

Fort Atkinson, Wisconsin

Acknowledgments

Thanks to:

The members of Lincoln Story League, a group of talented children's librarians and educators who are dedicated to introducing children to the delights of reading.

The following libraries for providing outstanding facilities and collections:
Arlington Heights Memorial Library, Barrington Area Library, Ela Area Library,
Mount Prospect Public Library, Palatine Area Library and Prospect Heights Public Library.

To the creative and talented people I worked with in the Youth Services Department of the Arlington Heights Memorial Library: Jeanne Achenbach, Marsha Balster, Pat Craig, Barbara d'Ambrosio, Maureen Dudle, Mary Ferrini, Ruth Griffith, Fred Gross, Margaret Kennedy, Gloria Kries, Betty Lockwood, Mary Lucas, Judy Moskal, Erika Scherf and Sara Zimmerman.

To these teachers who recognized my gifts and talents: Kerry Tomb, Bill Miller and Kathryn Jensen

To my beloved dog, Sweetbriar's Highland Lassie—"Briar" who reminds me that I need to take time to play and go for a long walk each day.

My late parents Donald and Jane Dingwall for instilling in me a love of reading and books.

Published by Alleyside Press, an imprint of Highsmith Press LLC
Highsmith Press
W5527 Highway 106
P.O. Box 800
Fort Atkinson, Wisconsin 53538-0800
1-800-558-2110

© Cindy Dingwall, 1998
Cover design: Frank Neu
Interior art: Heidi Green

Library of Congress Cataloging-in-Publication Data

  Dingwall, Cindy.
    Storybook birthday parties / Cindy Dingwall.
      p. cm.
    Includes bibliographical references (p.).
    ISBN 1-57950-015-3 (pbk. : alk. paper)
     1. Children's parties. 2. Literary recreation.
   3. Storytelling. 4. Education, Elementary--Activity
  programs. I. Title.
  GV1493.D52 1998
  793.2'1--dc21   97-44990
                                  CIP

Contents

Introduction

You're invited to share some wonderful birthday adventures with children. In this book you will find 30 birthday celebrations for famous children's book characters. The characters are those who have long lasting appeal to children. Several books have been written about each character, allowing children to enjoy a series of books about one individual.

The parties in this book can be used in public libraries, school libraries, classroom settings or park districts. Parents can use them for home parties.

This book has been divided into three sections: Age 3 – Kindergarten, Kindergarten – Grade 2 and Grades 3 – 5. There is some overlap in ages to allow for flexibility in programming. Each section has ten birthday parties, five parties for female characters and five for male characters.

Stories, songs, games, projects and activities are included at each party. Of course refreshments are an important part of each celebration. Let parents know that food will be served. Some children are on special diets. Be willing to make allowances and serve alternative snacks to those children. If necessary, allow parents to supply alternative snacks for their children.

The parties allow for active participation by children. Competitive games have been omitted to allow children to participate without having to worry about winners and losers.

Some of the books have videos and filmstrips available, however avoid using them unless absolutely necessary. Children need more live entertainment. Be aware that federal regulations often prohibit the use of videocassettes in public settings.

For those of you using these programs in public libraries or park districts, there is a sample registration card in the appendices on pp. 152–153. This card allows you to take a wide variety of information. Having information regarding age and grade level of each child will allow you to divide the children into smaller multi-age groupings for some of the activities. You may also want to include this information in your statistics when you make your written report of the program.

When presenting programs in public libraries and park districts, try to offer several sessions of each. Include morning, afternoon, evening and weekend times. This allows you to accommodate the various schedules of today's busy families. School holidays can be an especially good time to offer programs.

So that children do not tire of birthday celebration programs, it is recommended that you only do two birthday celebrations in each age group per year, perhaps one female and one male character each year. This schedule will provide you with several years of programming for each age group.

Read pp. 8 – 12 carefully before planning your celebrations. These pages contain important information for any party that you plan. Also, each section is preceded by an introduction that contains information you need before beginning to plan. On the next the few pages you will find more information that will help you.

Now, go celebrate and have fun!

Before You Begin

The information given here is basic to all of the parties in the book.

REGISTRATION

When doing these program in a public library or park district, use index cards to register children. See p. 152–153 for sample registration and waiting list cards.

SPACE NEEDS

You will need an area that allows space for children to sit on the floor and listen to stories and sing songs. Tables and chairs are needed for projects and snacks. Some of the parties have the children look around the room or children's department in the library to find something. Adapt these activities as needed.

MATERIALS DISPLAY

On the day of the program provide a display of materials about the character whose birthday you are celebrating. Encourage the children to enjoy looking at these books at school. Children coming to the library for the party can be encouraged to check these items out.

CAMERA AND FILM

Have a camera loaded with a 12-exposure roll of color film. Take photos of the program for display.

NAME TAGS

Each party has a special nametag. Neatly print the child's first and last name on the name tag. Name tags can be pinned to a child's clothing. An alternative is to print the name on both sides, punch a hole in the top of the tag and string it with yarn. You can also purchase name tags in teacher and party stores.

PRIZES

Some of the games have the children look for things. At other times each child wins a small prize for participating in the game. Adapt these activities to fit your needs.

PUZZLES

There is a puzzle that accompanies each party. Adapt the puzzle to make it simpler if necessary. For dot-to-dots it may be necessary to fill in the puzzle and let the younger children use it as a coloring page. Older children will be able to connect the dots. To simplify mazes, draw in the line children are to follow and have them draw over it with a crayon. Encourage parents and children to work on puzzles together.

STORY BAGS

Each of the parties includes a story bag. This is optional. It can be used to carry home the art projects made in the program, the prizes a child wins playing a game and the puzzles and materials lists you give to each child. For the Christina Katerina party the art project is a story box that the children take home.

Happy Celebrating!!!

Program Suggestions

1. When presenting these programs, adapt them to fit your needs. (Space, location, students abilities etc.)

2. When using the puzzles, adapt them to fit the needs of the students you work with. Coloring puzzles can be made easier by outlining portions to be colored with the appropriate color. More lines can be added to make puzzles more challenging. Try working on word puzzles in small groups or as a class.

3. Avoid thinking in terms of boy parties or girl parties. Both boys and girls can enjoy these parties together. Everyone needs to learn that both girls and boys can be in main character roles.

Supplementary Ideas

1. Write letters to the authors whose books you have enjoyed. Tell them why you like their books. Most authors will write back to children or classes who write. Send these letters to the authors via their publishers. Publisher addresses can be found in *Literary Marketplace* (RR Bowker).

2. Have the children learn more about the authors whose books you highlight. Use *Something About the Author* (Gale) or the *Meet the Authors and Illustrators* (Scholastic) series.

3. Have the children do book reports on the books from each program. They can do these individually or in cooperative learning groups.

4. Invite the children to prepare creative presentations of the books they read. They can make dioramas, murals, banners and more to highlight the books they enjoy. Display these for other students to enjoy.

5. Let the children write letters to the book characters you highlight in your programs. You can display these or send them to the author.

6. Have the children check Internet sites to see if these authors have home pages. One of the best sources for this information is the **Children's Literature Web Guide,** containing links to hundreds of websites. <http://www.ucalgary.ca/~dkbrown/index.html>

7. Invite authors to visit your school or library, perhaps to participate in a birthday celebration.

8. Have children do booktalks on the books they enjoy reading. Perhaps they can entice others to enjoy these books too.

9. Some of these books have been made into video cassettes. Watch them together and compare the video to the book. What is the same? What is different? Why do you think they needed to make changes when they made the video? What do you think of the actors who portray the characters?

10. Some of these books have audiocassettes. Listen to them. Are they readings or dramatizations? What do you like or dislike about them? Encourage children to listen to books on tape while traveling. They can be an enjoyable way to pass the time on long trips.

11. Has the author of the books you enjoyed in today's program written other books? If so, encourage the children to read them. Ask the children why they think the author wrote other kinds of books. Ask why they think the author wrote a series of books about the same character.

12. Write to the authors and ask for autographed photos. Create an "author alcove" in your library where you display pictures of these authors. You can include a short biography, a letter from the author and a list of books each has written next to their photo. Be sure to hang these at "child height."

Story Presentation

Booktalking: Booktalking is a way to entice children to read books. It's very simple to do. Select the books you wish to highlight. Then tell the story or incident up to the climax. Never reveal the outcome. Tell the children that if they want to know what happens next they will have to read the book. Caution those who have already read the book, that one never tells someone who hasn't read a book how it ends. Tell them they too can say, "You'll have to read the book."

Storytelling: It's fun to tell a story rather than read it. This way you have constant eye contact with the children. It does take time, work and practice to tell a story to an audience. Begin by summarizing the story. Tell someone about the story. Do this several times. Then begin telling it in your own words. You will never tell it exactly the same way twice, and that's as it should be. Avoid word for word memorization. It sounds memorized, and it is too easy to get lost in the middle. Practice telling the story to your friends, family and pets. Once you know a story, it becomes yours to share with others.

Creative Mixes: Be creative in how you present stories. Use flannel boards, story cards, props, tandem telling, dramatizations, etc. It's fun for everyone when you use a variety of methods to tell a story.

Publicity

Publicity is an important part of any program. Here are several effective ways to promote your programs:

- Have a large, eye-catching poster in the children's department. Suggestions for these are given with each program. You can also make similar posters to put in your entrance area.

- Provide individual flyers alongside each poster. People can take these home as reminders to sign up.

- Posters and flyers should include the following: Name of program, age group the program is for, time and date, registration date and time. If you require that people be your own library card holders state that as well. *(Ex: Children must be Glenfield Library Cardholders in order to register for and attend this program.)*

- If your library issues a newsletter, be sure the program information is included. If you don't have a mailing list, consider starting one. Use your cardholders records to begin a mailing list. Some libraries routinely send out newsletters to all households they serve, while others ask people to sign up to be on the mailing list.

- Send information to the people who prepare the school newsletters. Write a brief article about the program. This information can be sent to public, private and parochial schools served by your library. Ask them if they would be willing to include news about library events in their newsletters. Keep copies of the articles that appear in the school newsletters.

- Information also needs to be sent to area newspapers. Again, write a brief article about the program. Try to become acquainted with the newspaper people who are responsible for this area.

- Keep copies of all press releases that you send to schools and area newspapers. That way if there is a mistake, you can provide a copy with the correct information.

- Keep copies of all articles that appear about your program. This includes articles from the library newsletter, school newsletters and area newspapers.

- Begin a scrapbook that highlights all of your programs. Include the press releases, program flyers, photos of the poster and of course photos from each program you offer. It makes a nice momento and reminds you of what you have done.

Keep Your Program Running Smoothly

There must be discipline of a program is to run smoothly and be enjoyable for all who attend it. Children often misbehave because they are not aware of what is expected of them. This is easy to remedy. Make sure you let them know how they are to behave during a program.

When working with **preschoolers and kindergartners**, have the children enter the room and take a place on the floor. Have a tape of children's songs playing for them to listen to before the program begins.

When it is time to begin, start by welcoming them. Then explain how we behave. "When we listen to stories we have to be quiet. Everyone needs to sit on the floor with their legs crossed under them like this (show them). Now fold your hands like this (show them), and put them in your lap like this (show them). We have to remember not to talk to other people. We have to remember not to touch other people. That way everyone will enjoy the program." You may need to stop and remind young children from time to time.

Sometimes it is very effective to stop and look at those who are talking and wait.

Children who tell you they can't do it can be encouraged with the words, *"Sure you can."*

Try challenging children with the words, *"Let's see who can be the quietest listener."* Another phrase that works well is, *"Show me how quietly you can listen."*

If a child says, *"I don't want to,"* respond with, *"You have to. It's the rule."* Go on with the program. Avoid getting into discussions with children when it comes to discipline. Firmly state the rule and go on.

Sometimes parents may want to use program time as a time to visit. Explain that they too need to be attentive. *"Parents, I know it's tempting to visit with one another, but it's important for you to listen quietly as well. Set a good example for your child by not visiting with you neighbor. Sit and listen the way I asked the children to do. If your child begins to talk, put your finger to your lips like this to indicate silence (show them). If your child really doesn't feel like listening today, that's okay. Feel free to take them out of the room. There are some days when children just don't feel like sitting still and listening."*

A child who throws a temper tantrum must be removed immediately. They can return once they have regained control, or you can choose to have them remain out of the program.

Of course there are times when you want audience participation. Say, *"I need you to help me with this story. This is what I want you to do."* This is not to much to ask of children this age.

Preschoolers and kindergartners can learn to sit and listen quietly. It takes time and patience, but once they know what you expect and that you do expect it, they are usually cooperative. If children learn this important lesson now, it will become a good habit that they follow naturally.

When working with **older children**, invite them to sit in the seating area. Play a tape of children's songs or one of the author's stories that you won't be using in the program for them to listen to while waiting.

Stating the rules usually works well with older children. *"You probably know the rules of listening. When someone else is talking, you listen to them and remain quiet."* Elementary students are used to classroom behavior where they listen attentively while others are speaking. They know how to raise their hands when they wish to speak.

If you do run into problems with this age group, try saying, *"If you don't want to listen, you are free to leave. I'll call your parents later to explain why I asked you to leave the program."* Leave the choice up to the child. If a child does choose to leave, do call the parents and let them know what happened. Tell the child's parents that you are sorry their child did not enjoy the program. However, be firm in letting them know that disruptive behavior will not be tolerated. This kind of behavior is often a pattern with a particular child.

At the end of your program, thank the children for their cooperation. For younger children say, *"Thank you for being such good listeners today. You have very nice manners, and you were very cooperative."* If you do this consistently, you are likely to have few problems with discipline. For older kids say, *"Thanks for being so cooperative. it really helped a lot. I appreciate it. Tell your parents I said you have good manners."*

Again, if you are consistent with instructions and praise, it does work.

Children should never be allowed to tease, make fun of or physically harm one another. If this type of behavior occurs, immediately stop the program and firmly tell the children that this behavior is not allowed and will not be tolerated. In extreme cases, a child must be removed from the program. Always let a parent know when their child engages in such behavior. Be firm in letting parents know that this behavior will not and cannot be allowed. In extreme cases, it may be necessary to tell a child's parent that they can no longer attend programs unless there is a positive change of behavior.

Keep in mind that even the President of the United States of America and his family have what they call "Protocol Advisors" who tell them how to behave in different circumstances. Consider yourself a "Children's Protocol Advisor." If your school or library has a behavior policy, keep it on hand to show parents should they question you.

Parties for Preschool and Kindergarten Children

The parties in this section are for children ages three years through kindergarten. This would include children who turn six during their kindergarten year. Up to twenty children per group works well. You can work with one age group or a mixed age group depending upon your situation.

When doing these parties in a school setting, enlist the assistance of your "room parents." "Room parents" can work with small groups of children on the projects that call for assistance. School volunteers can also be asked to help.

For those of you presenting these programs in a public library setting, encourage the child's parent or guardian to attend the program with their child (ren). Let parents know that some of the activities require adult assistance. This also allows parents to see their child in a group setting. It offers them the opportunity to interact with their child (ren) and learn about enjoyable activities they can do at home. **When registering for these programs, let them know that an adult needs to attend with their child (ren).** Encourage parents to plan for alternative care for younger and older siblings. This allows parents to give the child (ren) they bring to the program their undivided attention. Let them know that alternative care does not mean leaving their other children unattended in the library. Consider enlisting the assistance of library volunteers for assistance with programs. They are often willing and eager helpers.

Some children may be hesitant to participate in a group activity. Let them observe. If a child prefers not to complete an art project, let them take it home to do there. Saying, *"That's okay. Sometimes, I would rather watch than take part too,"* helps them feel better. Reassure parents that this is normal behavior. When children feel comfortable, they will be willing to take a more active part. Even when watching, children are learning and gaining something worthwhile from an activity. Sometimes children just don't feel like doing something on a particular day, and that's okay.

Try to follow the order and format given for each party. You will notice that songs, games and activities relate to a particular story in each series. Young children have short attention spans and benefit from having a story followed by a song, game or project that relates to that story.

The objectives for these parties are as follows:
- Encourage an appreciation of literature and introduce children to some new story friends
- Increase listening skills
- Enhance creativity (art projects)
- Develop social skills in a group situation (taking turns at games)
- Develop problem solving skills

You're Invited!

Christina Katerina's Birthday Party!

Based on the books by Patricia Lee Gauch

Celebrate Christina Katerina's 5th Birthday: Program (45–60 minutes)

Story: *Christina Katerina and the Box* Read this story.
Use a large box as a prop.

Song: **"Christina Katerina Had a Great Big Box"** (Song on p. 14)
Make flannelboard figures of each of the things the box becomes.
Put each figure on the board as you sing about it.

Story: *Christina Katerina and the Great Bear Train* Read this story.

Game: **The Bear Train Game** (Instructions on p. 14.)

Project: **Decorate Your Story Box** (Instructions on p. 15.)

Snack: Light the candles on the cake and sing "Happy Birthday" to
Christina Katerina. Blow out the candles and make a wish.
Bring each person a piece of cake and a cup of juice.

Story Boxes: As the children leave the room, give
them their story boxes to take home.

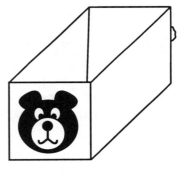

Planning and Promotion

Advertising Display: Place a large doll dressed like Christina Katerina in a box. Decorate the sides of the box with your program and registration announcements. Provide flyers that repeat this information for people to take home.

Room Decorations: Decorate the room for a birthday party, using balloons, banners and streamers. Display a variety of boxes that depict events in the stories. Choose a paper tablecloth, plates, cups and napkins that depict something from one of the stories or use any birthday-themed party goods.

Name Tags: Use the birthday present name tag on p. 15. Print the child's first and last name on the tag. An alternative is to print the child's name on both sides of the tag, punch a hole in the top and string it with yarn. Then tags can be slipped over the children's heads.

Snacks: Have a birthday cake with **HAPPY BIRTHDAY, CHRISTINA KATERINA** printed on it. Decorate cake the to depict something in one of the stories. Insert five candles on the top. Have fruit juice for the beverage.

Story Boxes: Each child will decorate a box to take home. Put a copy of the puzzle on p. 16 and a box-shaped materials list of the Christina Katerina materials in your library in each child's box. The children can take their boxes home, and put treasures inside them. If desired you can give party prizes: A box of crayons or chalk, a box of candy, teddy bear stickers, ballet stickers, etc.

Christina Katerina books by Patricia Lee Gauch

Books are listed in series order.

Christina Katerina and the Box. New York: Coward-McCann, 1971. Christina makes all sorts of wonderful things out of the box from the new refrigerator. But one day the box falls apart and has to be thrown away.

Christina Katerina and the First Annual Grand Ballet. New York: Coward-McCann & Geoghegan, 1973. Christina had quite an experience in the ballet.

Christina Katerina and the Time She Quit the Family. New York: Putnam, 1987. Christina was tired of her family, so she quit.

Christina Katerina and the Great Bear Train. New York: Putnam, 1990. Christina and her bears went for a walk around town. What adventures they had!

Christina Katerina and Fat's and the Great Neighborhood War. New York: Putnam, 1997. The trouble begins when Tommy Moorhouse moves in. A war breaks out among the kids in the neighborhood.

Song

Christina Katerina Had a Great Big Box
(Sung to: "Wheels on the Bus")

Christina Katerina had a great big box, a great big box, a great big box.
Christina Katerina had a great big box.
And she had lots of fun!

Christina made a castle from the great big box, the great big box, the great big box.
Christina made a castle from the great big box.
And she had lots of fun!

Christina made a clubhouse from the great big box, the great big box, the great big box.
Christina made a clubhouse from the great big box.
And she had lots of fun!

She made a racing car from the great big box, the great big box, the great big box.

She made a racing car from the great big box.
And she had lots of fun!

She made a summer mansion from the great big box, the great big box, the great big box.
She made a summer mansion from the great big box.
And she had lots of fun!

Her box fell apart and had to be thrown away, thrown away, thrown away.
Her box fell apart and had to be thrown away.
Does that mean no more fun?

Here comes her friend with another box, another box, another box.
Here comes her friend with another box.
Oh, they had lots of fun!

Instructions for Bear Train Walk Game

Materials

tape

train cars *Use flannelboard pattern books to make a variety of train cars. Decorate them all differently. Laminate or cover them with clear contact paper.*

one bear per child *Make each bear different or give each child a bear pattern to color. Print each child's name on his/her bear.*

blindfold *(for use with kindergarten children)*

laminating film and machine or clear contact paper

Prior to the program

Put the bear train on the wall at child height.

Directions

1. One at a time, give each child a bear.

2. Sing this song as children put their bears into the train cars. Tape the bear to the train. (Sung to: "Mary Had a Little Lamb")

   Put the bear in the train, in the train, in the train.
   Put the bear in the train. And watch him/her take a ride.

3. Let younger children choose where to put their bear. Kindergarten children can be blindfolded, turned three times and pointed in the direction of the train.

4. Children may take their bears home at the end of the program or you may choose to display the train for others to enjoy.

Instructions for Bear Story Box

Materials

glue

crayons

brown tempera paint and brushes

dishwashing liquid

One of each item below per child

shoe box

bear head pattern

large brown pom-pom

  Available in craft stores.

Prior to the program

Paint each box with brown tempera paint. Add a small amount of dishwashing liquid to the paint, so it will stick to the boxes. Allow twenty-four hours to dry.

Directions

Make story boxes as a group, one step at a time. Ask parents or assistants to provide help as needed.

1. Give each child a bear head pattern. Ask parents/assistants to print the child's name on the bear head.

2. Have the children color their bear heads.

3. Have the children glue the bear head to the box.

4. Give each child a brown pom-pom. Show the children how to glue the pom pom to the back of the box.

5. Let the boxes dry for the remainder of the program.

6. While the program continues, have your assistant put a puzzle and materials list into each box. If you are giving party prizes, these can be put in at this time.

7. Let children take the boxes home after the program.

Patterns

name tag

bear pattern for story box

The Bear Train Walk

Help Christina and her bear train make it home safely.

You're Invited!

Corduroy's Birthday Party!

Based on the books by Don Freeman

Celebrate Corduroy's 3rd Birthday: Program (45-60 minutes)

Story: *Corduroy*   Read this story.

Song: "Little Bear" (Song on p. 18)

Story: *A Pocket for Corduroy*   Read this story.

Activity: **A Pocket and Button Hunt** (Instructions on p. 18)

Project: **Make a Bear Puppet** (Instructions are on p. 19)

Snacks: Have the parents and children remain seated. Light the candles on the bear cookie and sing "Happy Birthday to Corduroy." Blow out the candles and make a wish. Bring each person one cookie and a cup of juice.

Story Bags: Give children their story bags as they leave.

Planning and Promotion

Advertising Display: Have a stuffed Corduroy Bear holding a sign that includes the program and registration information. Place flyers nearby with the same information for people to take home as reminders.

Room Decorations: Decorate the room with teddy bear pictures, streamers, balloons and banners that say HAPPY BIRTHDAY, CORDUROY! Try to find bear-themed paper tablecloth, plates, cups and napkins.

Puppet: Use the Corduroy Bear stuffed animal.

Name Tags: Use the bear pattern on p. 20. Print the child's first and last name on the tag. Pin the name tag to the child's clothing.

Snacks: Serve small bear-shaped cookies and juice. These can be purchased in the grocery store. Make a large bear cookie out of play dough. Decorate it. Insert three candles into the cookie.

Story Bags: Give each child a brown lunch sack with a teddy bear cutout attached that says: I'VE BEEN TO CORDUROY'S BIRTHDAY PARTY AT _____! Children can use these to carry home their art project, puzzle, and the materials list. You can add a bear bookmark if desired. Label bags with the children's names before the program. This allows you to put the child's puppet into the right bag later.

Corduroy books by Don Freeman

Books are listed in series order.

Corduroy. New York: Viking, 1968. Corduroy needs a new button for his overalls, so he sets out to find one. He doesn't find his button, but he finds something much more special.

A Pocket for Corduroy. New York: Viking, 1978. When Corduroy sets off in search of a pocket, he has some exciting and scary adventures.

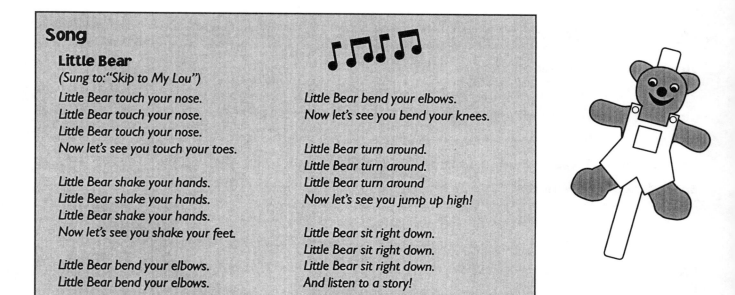

Song

Little Bear

(Sung to: "Skip to My Lou")

Little Bear touch your nose.
Little Bear touch your nose.
Little Bear touch your nose.
Now let's see you touch your toes.

Little Bear shake your hands.
Little Bear shake your hands.
Little Bear shake your hands.
Now let's see you shake your feet.

Little Bear bend your elbows.
Little Bear bend your elbows.

Little Bear bend your elbows.
Now let's see you bend your knees.

Little Bear turn around.
Little Bear turn around.
Little Bear turn around
Now let's see you jump up high!

Little Bear sit right down.
Little Bear sit right down.
Little Bear sit right down.
And listen to a story!

Instructions for Pocket and Button Hunt

Materials

1 small felt pocket per child *(pattern on p.19)*
1 button to go inside each pocket

Prior to the program

1. Use the pattern to cut out two pockets per child. You will want to make all of the pockets identical.

2. Glue or stitch the two pieces of felt together on three sides to make a pocket. Leave the top open.

3. Slip a button inside each pocket.

4. Hide the pockets

Directions

1. Show the children (and parents) a sample pocket.

2. Tell the children (and parents) to look for and find one pocket each. Tell them there is a surprise inside the pocket.

3. When they find the pocket, they can return to the seating area. Put the pockets aside. You will use them when you make the puppet.

Materials and Prep

Instructions for Bear Puppet

Materials

fabric glue *Have enough bottles so there is minimal sharing needed.*

black markers

One of each item below per child

button *Children found a second button on their hunt. Make sure all buttons are identical.*

paint stick

bear cutout (pattern on p. 20.)
  Use fuzzy brown fur or brown felt

set of movable eyes
  You can also use blue felt circles.

small brown pom-pom *This is for the nose. Black felt circles can be substituted.*

pink mouth (pattern on p. 20.)

felt pocket with button inside
  This is the one found during the hunt.

Prior to the program

Print each child's first and last name on a paint stick.

Directions

Make puppets as a group, one step at a time. Ask parents or assistants to provide help as needed.

1. Give each child a bear.

2. Give each child the eyes. Have them glue the eyes to the bear's face.

3. Give each child the nose. Have them glue the nose to the bear's face.

4. Give each child the mouth. Have them glue the mouth to the bear's face.

5. Give each child a pair of green, felt overalls. Have them glue the overalls to the bear.

6. Give each child a pocket. Tell them to take the button out. Glue the button to the right side of the overalls. Glue the pocket to the front of the overalls.

7. Give each child a paint stick. Have them glue the bear to the paint stick.

8. Put children's finished puppets into their story bags.

9. Encourage children to let the puppets dry overnight before using it.

Patterns

Pattern for overalls and pocket. See p. 20 for bear pattern.

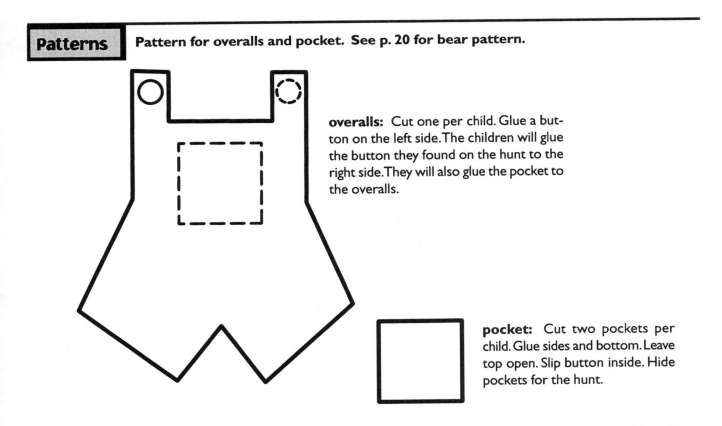

overalls: Cut one per child. Glue a button on the left side. The children will glue the button they found on the hunt to the right side. They will also glue the pocket to the overalls.

pocket: Cut two pockets per child. Glue sides and bottom. Leave top open. Slip button inside. Hide pockets for the hunt.

Bear pattern for name tag, story bag & puppet

Note: The bear and overalls (p.19) need to be drawn so the overalls fit the bear when cut out.

mouth

Something's Lost

Oh no! The little bear has lost his pocket and his button. Help him find them. Then have him go home. Be sure to follow the path.

You're Invited!

Nora's Birthday Party!

Based on the books by Satomi Ichikawa

Celebrate Nora's 5th Birthday: Program (45-60 minutes)

I've been to Nora's birthday party at

Story: *Nora's Stars*   Make this into a flannelboard story.

Project: **Star Pictures** (Instructions on p. 23)

Story: *Nora's Roses* Read this story.

Game: **Put the Roses on the Vine** (Instructions on p. 23)

Story: *Nora's Castle* Read this story.

Snacks: Light the candles on the cake and sing "Happy Birthday" to Nora. Blow out the candles and make a wish. Bring each person a piece of cake and a cup of juice.

Story Bags: Give children their story bags as they leave. Make sure their Star Pictures are inside.

Planning and Promotion

Advertising Display: Have a dark blue poster board with a castle on it. Have shiny stars in the sky. Have the program and registration information on the poster. Provide star shaped flyers with the program and registration information for people to take as reminders.

Room Decorations: Have a castle door on the door to the room where you will hold the party. Try to decorate the inside to look like the inside of Nora's castle. Have all of her friends there too: Maggie the doll, Teddy the bear, Kiki the dog, and the guests who came to Nora's castle party. Try to find a tablecloth, plates, napkins and cups with a castle theme.

Name Tags: Use the star pattern on p. 23. Trace it on to silver paper.

Snacks: Have a birthday cake with a castle drawn on it. Print **HAPPY BIRTHDAY, NORA** on it. Drink pink lemonade.

Story Boxes: Give each child a white lunch sack with a silver star attached. Print **I'VE BEEN TO NORA'S BIRTHDAY PARTY AT** _____ on the star. Children can use these to carry home their Star Pictures, a star-shaped list of the Nora materials in your library, and the puzzle on p. 24. Prizes can include: rose stickers and other items you find that are related to the stories.

Nora books by Satomi Ichikawa

Books are listed in series order.

Nora's Castle. New York: Philomel, 1984. Nora decides to visit the castle she sees from her house.

Nora's Stars. New York: Philomel, 1989. Nora wants all of the stars in the sky, so a dancing doll flies into the sky and gets them for her.

Nora's Duck. New York: Philomel, 1991. Nora finds an injured duck and takes it to Doctor John who promises to help it heal.

Nora's Roses. New York: Philomel, 1993. Nora has a beautiful rose vine outside her window. But everyone keeps taking the flowers. One day there are no more roses on her vine.

Nora's Surprise. New York: Philomel, 1994. Nora receives a wonderful surprise from a sheep.

Instructions for Making Star Pictures

Materials

1 piece of dark blue construction
   paper per child

black markers

star stickers

Directions

Ask parents and other helpers to assist.

1. Give each child a piece of paper with his/her name printed on the bottom of it.

2. Give each child a sheet of star stickers.

3. Show the children how to stick the stars to the paper to make a "night sky."

4. Let the children take these home.

Patterns

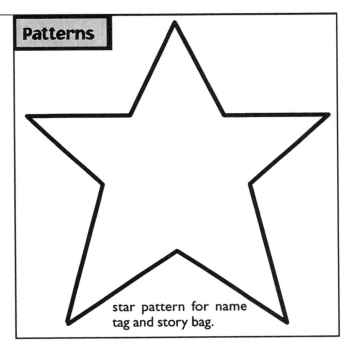

star pattern for name
tag and story bag.

Instructions for Put the Roses on the Vine

Materials

1 white trellis

green vines *(either artificial or made from paper)*

1 pink rose per child *(artificial or from tissue paper)*

blindfold *(optional)*

Prior to the program

1. Attach the vines to the trellis and secure them.

2. Prop the trellis against the wall.

Directions

1. Have the children sit on the floor facing the trellis.

2. Explain that you are going to help put the roses back on Nora's vine.

3. One at a time, have each child come forward. (If children choose to, they can put on the blindfold.)

4. Give the child a rose and tell him/her to find a place on the vine for it. Sing this song: "Put the Roses on the Vine" (Sung to: "Clementine.").

   Put the roses, put the roses, put the roses on the vine
   Look at our vine, it's so pretty, put the roses on the vine.

5. Put the trellis in a location where it will be enjoyed by all. You can set up a display of books about flowers and gardens by your lovely trellis.

Who Gave Nora a Surprise?

Read *Nora's Surprise* to get the answer.

You're Invited!

Peter's Birthday Party!

Based on the books by Ezra Jack Keats

Celebrate Peter's 6th Birthday: Program (45-60 minutes)

Story: *The Snowy Day* Read this story.

Song: "Let's Go for a Walk in the Snow" (Song on p. 26)

Project: Snow Pictures (Instructions on p. 26)

Game: Pass the Snowball Game (Instructions on p. 27)

Story: *A Letter to Amy* Read this story.
Use a mailbox and letters as props.

Snacks: Light the candles on the cake and sing "Happy Birthday" to Peter. Blow out the candles and make a wish. Bring each person a piece of cake and cup of juice.

Story Bags: Give each child a story bag as he/she leaves the room. Be sure their game prize is inside. Let them take their Snow Pictures home too.

Planning and Promotion

Advertising Display: Have a poster with Peter walking in the snow. He can be carrying a sign with the program and registration information printed on it. Provide snow-boot-shaped flyers with the program and registration information for people to take as reminders.

Room Decorations: Decorate the room for a birthday party. Try to find birthday decorations that remind you of Peter and some of his adventures.

Name Tags: Use the balloon pattern on p. 27.

Snacks: Have a white birthday cake with snowy white frosting. Decorate it with balloons. Print "Happy Birthday, Peter" on it. Have hot chocolate for the beverage.

Story Bags: Give each child a bag with a balloon shape attached that says, I'VE BEEN TO PETER'S BIRTHDAY PARTY AT _____. The children can put the prize they win playing the game on p. 27, the puzzle on p. 28 and a balloon-shaped list of the Peter stories owned by your library. Party prizes can include party horns and poppers.

Peter books by Ezra Jack Keats

Books are listed in series order.

The Snowy Day. New York: Viking, 1962. Peter has fun playing in the snow.

Whistle for Willie. New York: Viking, 1964. Peter keeps trying to learn how to whistle, so he can call his dog.

Peter's Chair. New York: Viking, 1967. Peter doesn't want his baby sister to have his chair, so he takes it back.

A Letter to Amy. New York: Harper, 1968. Peter decides to invite a girl to his birthday party.

Song

Let's Go for a Walk in the Snow
(Sung to: "Skip to My Lou")
Do the motions suggested in each verse. You can also add other movements that are in the story

Let's go for a walk in the snow.
Let's go for a walk in the snow.
Let's go for a walk in the snow.
We'll have lots of fun.

Let's turn our feet out, just like this.
Let's turn our feet out, just like this.
Let's turn our feet out, just like this.
We'll have lots of fun.

Let's drag our feet through the deep, deep snow.
Let's drag our feet through the deep, deep snow.

Let's drag our feet through the deep, deep snow.
We'll have lots of fun.

Let's lie down and make snow angels.
Let's lie down and make snow angels.
Let's lie down and make snow angels.
We'll have lots of fun.

Let's go back inside and sit down quietly.
Let's go back inside and sit down quietly.
Let's go back inside and sit down quietly.
We had lots of fun.

Instructions for Snow Pictures

Materials

dark blue heavy construction paper or cardboard

white shaving cream

newspapers and towels

spoons

markers

Directions

Do this as a group, one step at a time.

1. Give each child a piece of blue paper or cardboard.
2. Have parents (or helpers) print each child's name on the paper.
3. Give each child a large spoonful of shaving cream.
4. Let children use their fingers and hands to create a "snowy picture."
5. Let pictures dry flat for remainder of program.
6. Children may take these home.

Instructions for Pass the Snowball

Materials

1 white ball

1 bucket of party prizes *(whistles)*

1 audiocassette of children's songs

audiocassette player

Directions:

1. Have the children sit in a circle on the floor.

2. Give the snowball to one child.

3. Play the music. As the music plays the children pass the snowball around the circle.

4. When the music stops, the child holding the snowball leaves the circle. That child takes a prize out of the bucket.

5. Continue playing until all children have a prize.

Patterns

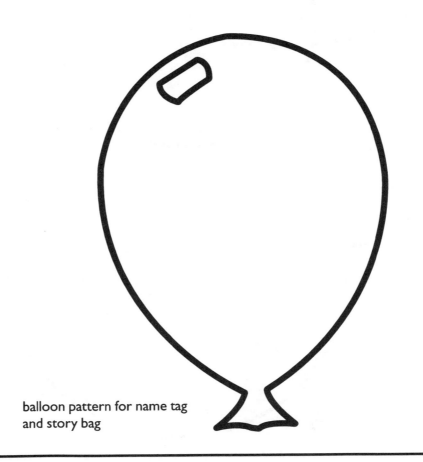

balloon pattern for name tag and story bag

What did Peter build?

Color the Bs blue to find the answer.

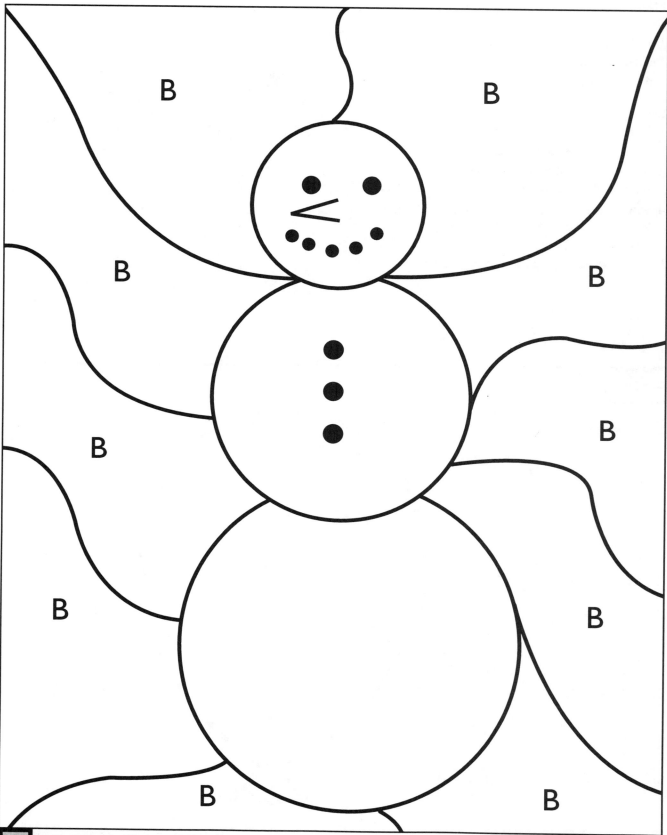

You're Invited!

Harold's Birthday Party!

Based on the books by Crockett Johnson

Celebrate Harold's 4th Birthday: Program (45-60 minutes)

Story: *Harold and the Purple Crayon* Read this story.

Treasure Hunt: **Find the Purple Crayons** (Instructions on p. 30)

Story: *A Picture for Harold's Room* Read this story.

Song: "Harold Had a Purple Crayon" (Song on p. 30)

Project: **Draw a Purple Picture for Your Room** (Instructions on p.31)

Story: *Harold's Fairy Tale* Present this as a "tell and draw story." Prior to the program, use pencil to lightly draw some of the pictures from the story onto paper. As you tell the story, use a purple crayon to draw over your lines. You can have some of the pictures already to go, and just put them up at the appropriate time. You only need to do a few for it to be effective.

Snacks: Light the candles and sing "Happy Birthday" to Harold. Blow out the candles and make a wish. Bring everyone a piece of cake and a cup of juice.

Story Bags: Let children take home their story bags. They can put their pictures inside of them.

Planning and Promotion

Advertising Display: Make a large cutout of Harold holding a purple crayon. He is writing the program information on a large poster. The writing should be done in purple crayon and resemble a child's printing. Mount the white board onto purple poster board. Provide lavender crayon-shaped flyers with the program information for people to take home.

Room Decorations: Decorate the room to look like Harold's bedroom. Refrain from having wall decorations other than the window. Add birthday banners, purple streamers and purple balloons. Try to find a lavender tablecloth. Glue purple paper crayons to it. If possible, use purple paper plates, cups and napkins.

Name Tags: Use the crayon pattern on p. 31. Copy it onto lavender paper and use a purple felt tip marker to print the child's first and last name on their tag.

Snacks: Make a crayon-shaped cake. Have one 9" x 13" cake and one 12" square cake. Cut the square cake in half so you have two triangles. Join the rectangle and one triangle to make a crayon. Frost with white or lavender frosting. Write **HAPPY BIRTHDAY, HAROLD** with purple gel. Put four purple crayons in the cake. Serve with purple juice.

Story Bags: Have one white lunch sack per child. Attach a purple crayon (p. 31) that says **I'VE BEEN TO HAROLD'S BIRTHDAY PARTY AT** _____. Party prizes can include: a large purple crayon and several sheets of white paper, the puzzle on p. 32, and a purple crayon-shaped booklist of the Harold books available in your library.

Harold books by Crockett Johnson

Books are listed in series order.

Harold and the Purple Crayon. New York: Harper, 1955. Harold takes his purple crayon when he goes for a walk one night.

Harold's Trip to the Sky. New York: Harper, 1957. Harold and his purple crayon take an awesome trip to the sky.

Harold's Circus. New York: Harper, 1959. Harold and his purple crayon have an amazing adventure at the circus.

A Picture for Harold's Room. New York: Harper, 1960. Harold needs a picture for his room. And what a wonderful picture he draws!

Harold's ABC. New York: Harper, 1963. Harold's purple crayon takes him on an alphabetical journey to the moon.

Harold's Fairy Tale. New York: HarperCollins, 1984. Harold and his purple crayon draw an enchanted forest where he meets a giant witch.

Song

Harold Had a Purple Crayon

(Sung to: "Mary Had a Little Lamb")
As you sing this together, put purple drawings of each thing Harold draws on the flannelboard. You can create additional verses if desired.

Harold had a purple crayon, purple crayon, purple crayon.
Harold had a purple crayon, and he drew lots of pictures.

One night Harold drew a dragon, drew a dragon, drew a dragon.
One night Harold drew a dragon. It was mean and fierce.

Harold drew a ship and whale, ship and whale, ship and whale.
Harold drew a ship and whale, they both were in the sea.

He drew a picture for his room, for his room, for his room.
He drew a picture for his room, and put it on the wall.

Instructions for Find the Purple Crayons

Materials
1 large purple crayon per child
1 empty crayon box

Prior to the program
Hide the crayons for the children to find.

Directions
1. Tell the children to look for and find one purple crayon.

2. When they find the crayons, they bring them to you and put them inside your box.

   Hint: Provide assistance as needed. Make sure each child finds only one crayon.

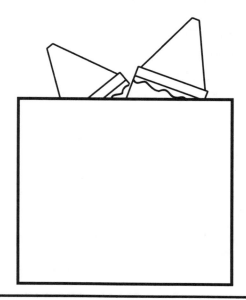

Instructions for Draw a Purple Picture for Your Room

Materials
I purple crayon per child
These were found on the "crayon hunt."

I piece of white construction paper per child (9" x 11")

I piece of purple construction paper per child (10" x 12")

rubber cement

tape or fish net and clothes pins
(if you choose to display)

Directions
1. Explain that you are going to draw pictures for Harold's room. The group will put the pictures on the wall for everyone to enjoy.

2. Give each child a piece of white paper.

3. Let the children use the purple crayons to draw their pictures.

4. When they are finished, use rubber cement to glue the pictures to the purple paper.

5. Use purple marker to print each child's name in the lower left corner of the picture.

6. Hang the pictures for all to see. Tell children they may take their pictures home when the program is over.

Hint: An effective and easy way to display pictures is to attach a large piece of fish net to the wall. You may be able to hang it from the ceiling, so it hangs against the wall. Another option is to staple it to the wall. It should reach the floor. Use clothes pins to attach pictures.

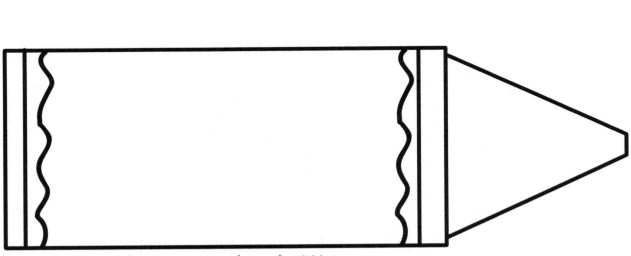

crayon for name tag, story bag and activities

What did you draw?

Use your purple crayon to connect the dots and make pictures of things Harold drew with his purple crayon.

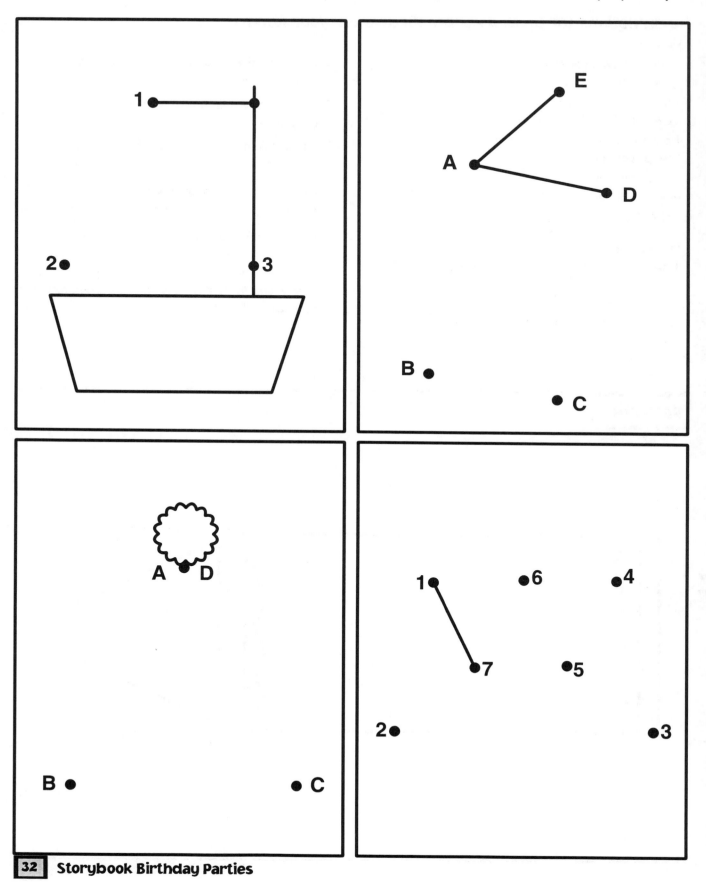

You're Invited!

Bill Crocodile's Birthday Party!

Based on the books by Tomie de Paola

Celebrate Bill's 5th Birthday: Program (45–60 minutes)

Story: ***Bill and Pete*** Read this story.

Activity: **Crocodile Hunt** (Instructions on p. 35)

Story: ***Bill and Pete Go Down the Nile*** Make this into a flannelboard.

Game: **Feed the Crocodile** (Instructions on p. 34)

Project: **Crocodile Mobile** (Instructions on p. 34)

Snacks: Light the candles on the cake. Sing "Happy Birthday" to Bill. Blow out the candles and make a wish. Bring each person a piece of cake and a cup of juice.

Story Bags: Give children their story bags to take home.

Planning and Promotion

Advertising Display: Create a large crocodile out of green poster board. Have it holding a sign with the program and registration information printed on it. Provide crocodile-shaped flyers for people to take as reminders.

Room Decorations: Try to find decorations on a crocodile theme. Add birthday balloons, banners and streamers.

Guest Character: Try to rent or make a crocodile costume. Have someone dress up in the costume and portray a crocodile. He can tell the children that he is Bill's friend.

Name Tags: Use the crocodile pattern on p. 35. Run it on green paper.

Snacks: Have a birthday cake with a drawing of a crocodile on top. Write **HAPPY BIRTHDAY, BILL CROCODILE** on it. Put five green candles in the cake. Serve "Green River Juice" (green Kool-Aid) for the beverage.

Story Bags: Have large, paper grocery sacks with a green crocodile cutout attached. Print **I'VE BEEN TO BILL CROCODILE'S BIRTHDAY PARTY AT** _____ on the crocodile. Use the pattern on p. 35. Children can use the bags to carry their project, the puzzle on p. 36, and a crocodile-shaped list of the Bill materials your library owns. They will also use it to carry home the materials they discover on the Crocodile Hunt. Party prizes can include: anything related to crocodiles (stickers, buttons with a crocodile on them, etc.)

Bill books by Tomie dePaola

Books are listed in series order.

Bill and Pete. New York: Putnam, 1978. One day William Everett Crocodile makes a new friend named Pete.

Bill and Pete Go Down the Nile. New York: Putnam, 1987. Bill and Pete have an exciting field trip exploring the Nile River.

Instructions for Feed the Crocodile

Materials

Bill Crocodile *(your guest character)*

1 bucket

1 beanbag per child

1 crocodile or birthday sticker per child

Directions

1. Have Bill stand and hold the bucket.

2. Bill can tell the children he knows some hungry crocodiles in the jungle. "Try to toss a bag of food into the bucket. I'll take the bucket of food to the jungle and give it to the crocodiles."

3. Let each child have a turn tossing a bag into the bucket.

4. When a child gets a bag in, they get a crocodile sticker.

5. Vary the distance from the bucket based on children's ages.

> ### Song
>
> **Feed the Crocodiles** ♪ ♪♪ ♪
> (Sung to: "Shoo-Fly")
>
> *Crocodiles are hungry, let's feed them.*
> *Crocodiles are hungry, let's feed them.*
> *Crocodiles are hungry, let's feed them.*
> *Give lots of food to the crocodiles.*
>
> *Toss in the food, just like this.*
> *Toss in the food, just like this.*
> *Toss in the food, just like this.*
> *Give lots of food to the crocodiles.*
>
> Alternate singing each verse until all of the food has been tossed into the bucket.

Instructions for Crocodile Mobile

Materials

paper punch

crayons

black felt markers

movable eyes *(optional)*

glue *(if using movable eyes)*

One of each item below per child

crocodile cutout *(pattern on p. 35.)* from cover/card stock paper

colored balloon cutout *(pattern on p. 35)* from cover/card stock paper

12" strand of yarn

6" strand of yarn

Prior to the program

1. Use thick, black marker to print **HAPPY BIRTHDAY, PETE** on the front and back of each balloon.

2. Punch a hole in the top and bottom of each balloon and in the top of the crocodile.

Directions

Do this as a group, one step at a time. Ask parents to help their own child [ren].

1. Give each child a balloon to color. They can color it any way they wish.

2. Let the children glue or color eyes on the crocodile.

3. Let children color the nose and mouth on their crocodiles.

4. Help children string their mobiles. The balloon goes on top. The crocodile goes under the balloon.

Instructions for Crocodile Hunt

Materials

1 large, paper grocery bag per child

Crocodile cut outs in six colors (green, yellow, blue, red, orange, purple—Make five of each color. Use the name tag pattern below.)

Prior to the program

1. Print each child's name on a grocery bag.

2. Place one crocodile of each color in each of the following areas: E/FICTION, E/NON-FICTION, CHILDREN'S MAGAZINES, AUDIO VISUAL, AND THE CHECK OUT DESK. Vary the locations of the crocodiles within the same location (for example: Those in the E FICTION could be by different authors, Those in the E/NON-FICTION section could be in different subject areas.)

3. Next to each crocodile, have a sign that tells the children what to do.

- Choose one book from this shelf and put it in your bag.

- Choose one audiocassette and put it in your bag.

- Choose one magazine and put it in your bag.

- Now you are at the Check Out Desk. Give your bag to the person at the desk. Give them your library card. Check out the materials in your bag.

Directions

1. Divide the children into groups of three-four children each. There will need to be one helper per group. If doing this with parents present, each parent will be asked to help their own child (ren).

2. Tell each group what color crocodile to look for. When they find the crocodile, he will tell them what to do.

3. When they are finished with the Crocodile Hunt, they can return to the program area.

4. When the children return, set the bags aside. They can take them home at the end of the program. Be sure bags are labeled with each child's name.

Note: *This is a way to acquaint children (and parents) with the different kinds of materials the library has for children. It helps them to begin to learn to look for and find something in the library.*

Hint: *If you are doing this program in a classroom, adapt it to fit your needs. Have the children look for various things hidden in the classroom. Use one color crocodile and tell them to look for things hidden by the crocodiles. Another option is to hide crocodile cut outs and let the children look for those to put in their bags. Each child who finds a crocodile can be given a small prize.*

Patterns

balloon

crocodile for name tag story bag and mobile

Who is it?

Color Gs green and Ys yellow.

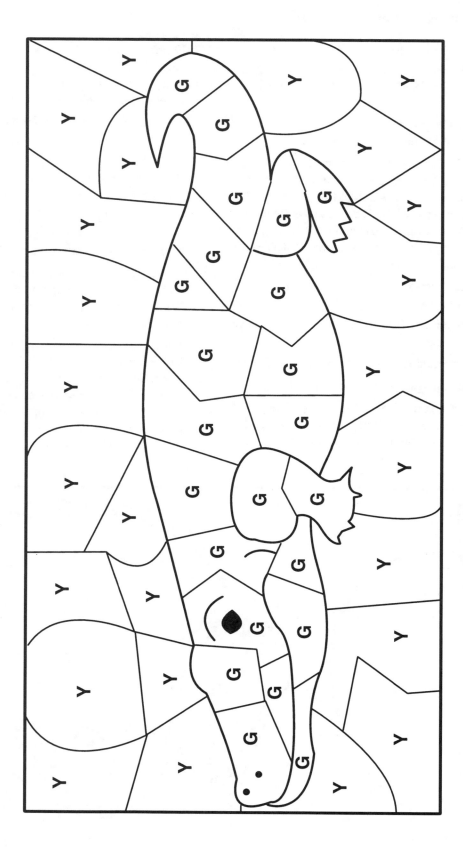

You're Invited!

Louanne Pig's
Birthday Party!

Based on the books by Nancy Carlson

Celebrate Louanne's 5th Birthday: Program (45-60 minutes)

Story: ***Louanne Pig and the Perfect Family***
If you use a pig puppet, let her help tell the story.

Project: **Piggy Paintings** (Instructions on p. 38)

Story: ***Louanne Pig and Making the Team*** Read this story.

Game: **Pig to Pig** (Instructions on p. 39)

Story: ***Louanne Pig and the Talent Show***
Make this into a flannelboard story.

Song: **Louanne Pig Was a Funny Pig** (Song on p. 38)

Snacks: Light the No. 5 candle on Louanne's cupcake. Sing "Happy Birthday" to her. Blow out the candles. Bring each person a cupcake and a cup of lemonade.

Story Bags: Give chidlren their story bags as they leave. They may take their pig paintings home too.

Planning and Promotion

Advertising Display: Make a large pig cutout and put the program and registration information on it. Provide pig-shaped flyers with the program and registration information for people to take as reminders.

Room Decorations: Try to find pig-themed decorations. Decorate for a birthday party using streamers, banners and balloons. Try to find pig-themed tablecloth, plates, cups and napkins. Have pictures of pigs on the walls. Ask staff to share pig stuffed animals they have.

Puppet: Try to find a pig puppet to use during the program.

name Tags: Use the pig-shaped name tag pattern on p. 39.

Snacks: Have pig cupcakes. Use any white cupcake recipe. Frost with pink frosting. Use small pieces of candy for the features. Lifesavers make good noses and M&Ms make good eyes. Use triangle-shaped candies for ears. Use thin-tipped tube frosting to make a squiggly tail. Put a No. 5 candle into Louanne's cupcake. Serve with pink lemonade.

Story Bags: Have brown lunch sacks. Attach a pink, pig-shaped cut out with the words, I'VE BEEN TO LOUANNE PIG'S BIRTHDAY PARTY AT _____ . Children can use these to carry home the puzzle on p.41, the pig mask they win playing the game, Pig to Pig on p. 40 and the pig-shaped list of Louanne Pig materials available in your library. Party prizes can include: A heart-shaped piece of pink or red paper that says, "You're Secret Admirer," and anything else that is pig related such as pig noses or pig pins.

Louanne Pig books by Nancy Carlson

Books are listed in series order.

Louanne Pig in the Perfect Family. New York: Carolrhoda, 1985. Louanne Pig thinks it would be fun to have lots of brothers and sisters, until she visits a friend.

Louanne Pig and Making the Team. New York: Carolrhoda, 1985. Louanne Pig tries out for the cheerleading squad. Her friend Arnie tries out for the football team. What a surprise they get!

Louanne Pig in the Talent Show. New York: Carolrhoda, 1985. Louanne takes part in the talent show.

Louanne Pig and the Witch Lady. New York: Carolrhoda, 1985. Louanne Pig manages to make friends with the neighborhood witch lady.

Louanne Pig in the Mysterious Valentine. New York: Puffin, 1987. Louanne Pig wants to know who sent her the Valentine signed, "You're Secret Admirer."

Song

Louanne Pig Was a Funny Pig
(Sung to: "Mary Had a Little Lamb")

Louanne Pig was a funny pig, funny pig, funny pig.
Louanne Pig was a funny pig, and she had lots of fun!

Louanne Pig wanted brothers and sisters, brothers and sisters, brothers and sisters.
Louanne Pig wanted brothers and sisters until she visited her friend.

She wanted to be a cheerleader, cheerleader, cheerleader
She wanted to be a cheerleader, but played football instead.

Louanne Pig was in the talent show, talent show, talent show
Louanne Pig was in the talent show. Oh, what fun she had!

Instructions for Piggy Paintings

Materials

1 large pig-shaped piece of butcher paper per child

1 small painting sponge per child *(Try to find pig-shaped sponges.)*

brown tempera paint. *Use powered paint and mix so it is quite thick.*

brown felt markers

disposable pie tins

painting smocks or old "daddy shirts"

Directions

Do this as a group, one step at a time.

1. Place the disposable pie tins with paint on the tables.

2. Give each child a paper pig.

3. Use brown marker to print child's first and last name on their pig.

4. Give each child a sponge and show them how to make sponge prints. Dip the sponge into the paint, and dab it on the paper so the sponge shape shows.

5. Try not to smear the sponges around.

6. Let dry. Children can take them home.

   Note: *Younger children might be more inclined to smear the sponges around on the paper. That's okay. The older children will be able to do the dabbing and lifting.*

Instructions for Pig to Pig Game

Materials

pig pattern (below)

heavy pink or flesh colored poster board

laminating machine and laminating film or clear contact paper

scissors

tape of children's songs and audiocassette player (If you can find pig songs, transfer them to a blank tape to use in the game.)

pig masks (pattern on p. 40)

Prior to the program

1. Enlarge pig pattern so it is very large. (Make one per child.)
2. Cut out and laminate (or cover with clear contact)
3. Make the "pig pen" by sectioning off an area of the room.

Directions

1. Have each child stand on a pig.
2. Play the music. Have children walk around the room.
3. Stop the music. Tell the children to find a pig to stand on. Do this several times, so they get the idea.
4. Now, remove one pig and put it in the "pig pen."
5. Play the music. Stop the music. Tell children to find a pig to stand on. One child will be without a pig. Tell that child to look in the pig pen. They stay there and walk around saying "Oink, Oink" very softly while the others continue.
6. Continue playing until all children are in the "pig pen." You may have to enlarge your "pig pen" as it gets more crowded. The kids in the pig pen can continue to play the game.
7. When all children are in the "pig pen" give each one a pig mask. Tell them you will put them into their story bags to take home.

Patterns

pig pattern for name tag, story bag and Pig to Pig game

Pig Mask

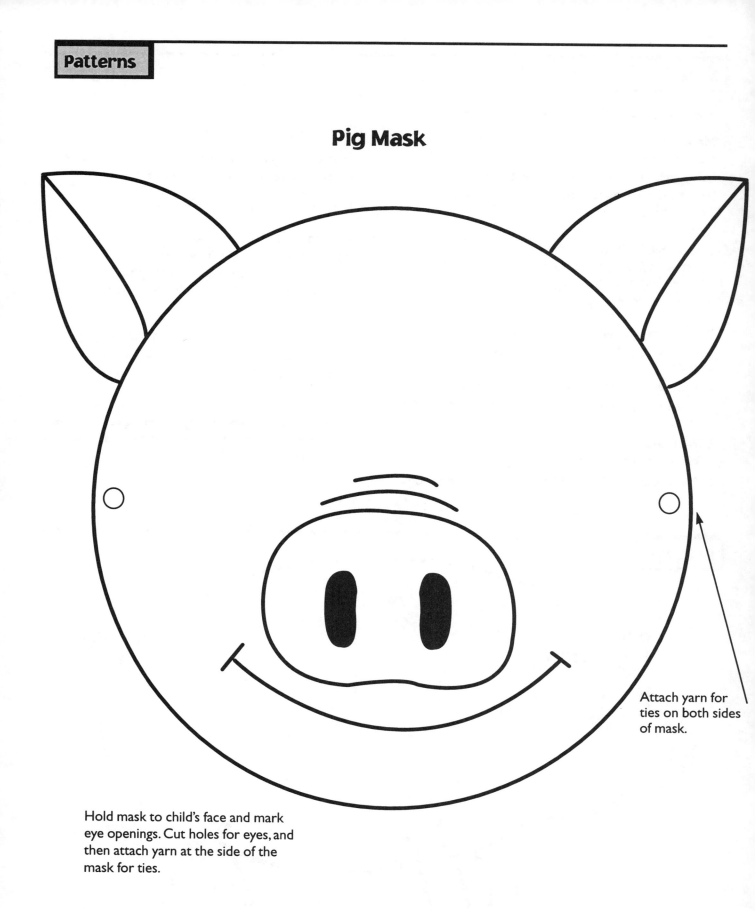

Attach yarn for ties on both sides of mask.

Hold mask to child's face and mark eye openings. Cut holes for eyes, and then attach yarn at the side of the mask for ties.

Where could they be?

Louanne Pig lost five Valentines. Can you help her find them?
Color each Valentine red when you find it.

You're Invited!

Miffy Rabbit's Birthday Party!

Based on the books by Dick Bruna

Celebrate Miffy's 3rd Birthday: Program (45-60 minutes)

Story: *Miffy* Read this story. You can wrap Miffy in a baby blanket.

Song: **Hop Like a Bunny!** (Song on p. 43)

Story: *Miffy at the Seashore* Use props to tell this story.

Project: **Rabbit Puppets** (Instructions on p. 44)

Story: *Miffy at the Zoo* Make this story into a flannelboard.

Game: **Put the Animals in the Zoo** (Instructions on p. 43)

Story: *Miffy's Birthday* Use the rabbit puppet to help tell this story. Have one box for each present in the story. Wrap each in different birthday paper. Wrap the top and bottom separately. This allows you to lift off the lid as you tell the story. Ask the children to guess what is inside each present.

Snacks: Light the candles on the cake and sing "Happy Birthday" to Miffy. Blow out the candles and make a wish. Bring each person a piece of cake and a cup of lemonade.

Story Bags: Give children their story bags as they leave.

Planning and Promotion

Advertising Display: Have a cutout of Miffy Rabbit next to a sign that has the program and registration information printed on it. Include rabbit-shaped flyers with the program and registration information printed on them.

Room Decorations: Try to find rabbit-themed decorations including a paper tablecloth, napkins, plates and cups. Have balloons, streamers and banners. Include stuffed animals that represent Miffy's friends.

Puppet: Have a white rabbit puppet. She can help tell some of the stories.

Name Tags: Use the rabbit pattern on p. 45.

Snacks: Have a rabbit-shaped birthday cake. Rabbit-shaped cake molds are available in craft stores, or you can make a rabbit cake from two round cakes as shown on p. 45. Frost with white frosting and cover with coconut. Use jelly beans for the features. Thin black licorice strands can be used for the whiskers. Put three candles into the cake. Have lemonade for the beverage.

Story Bags: Have a white lunch sack with a rabbit head glued on the front. Glue a white pom-pom on the back for the tail. Have a sign under the rabbit that says, **I'VE BEEN TO MIFFY RABBIT'S BIRTHDAY PARTY AT _____.** Children can use these to carry home their art project, the puzzle on p. 46 and their booklist. Party prizes can include: a sea shell, a plastic airplane, rabbit stickers and other rabbit related items.

Miffy books by Dick Bruna

Books are listed in series order.

Miffy. New York: Price Stern Sloan, 1984. Mr. and Mrs. Rabbit's wish for a baby bunny is finally granted.

Miffy at the Playground. New York: Price Stern Sloan, 1984. Miffy's parents take her to the playground.

Miffy at the Seashore. New York: Price Stern Sloan, 1984. Miffy and her dad have fun at the beach.

Miffy at the Zoo. New York: Price Stern Sloan, 1984. Miffy's dad takes her to the zoo.

Miffy Goes Flying. New York: Price Stern Sloan, 1984. Miffy's pilot uncle takes her for ride in his airplane.

Miffy Goes to School. New York: Price Stern Sloan, 1984. Miffy learns many new things at school.

Miffy in the Hospital. New York: Price Stern Sloan, 1984. Miffy has to go to the hospital to have her tonsils out.

Miffy in the Snow. New York: Price Stern Sloan, 1984. Miffy helped a bird who was trapped in the snow.

Miffy's Birthday. New York: Price Stern Sloan, 1984. Miffy has a birthday party.

Miffy's Dream. New York: Price Stern Sloan, 1984. Miffy has fun with a new friend.

Song

Hop Like a Bunny!

(Sung to: "Skip to My Lou")

Wiggle your bunny nose just like this.
Wiggle your bunny nose just like this.   [Wiggle noses.]
Wiggle your bunny nose just like this.
Let's see you wiggle your bunny nose.

Chew your carrots, just like this.
Chew your carrots, just like this.   [Chew carrots]
Chew your carrots, just like this.
Let's see you chew your carrots.

Twitch your bunny ears, just like this.
Twitch your bunny ears, just like this.
[Use hands to make bunny ears & twitch them.]

Twitch your bunny ears, just like this.
Let's see you twitch your bunny ears.

Hop like a bunny, just like this.
Hop like a bunny, just like this.   [Hop like bunnies.]
Hop like a bunny, just like this.
Let's see you hop like a bunny.

Sit down quietly, listen to a story.
Sit down quietly, listen to a story.
Sit down quietly, listen to a story.
Let's see you sit down quietly.
[Children sit down and listen quietly.]

Instructions for Put the Animals in the Zoo Game

Materials

Create a large zoo mural to put on the wall. Include cages, but no animals.

cutouts of 20 different zoo animals

1 empty box

Prior to the program

1. Put the animals cutouts in the box
2. Hang the mural at child height.

Directions

1. Have children come up one at a time.
2. Hold the box above the child's head and have the child reach in and pull out an animal. Say, "What animal did you pick?"
3. Have the child decide where to put their animal on the mural. Sing "Put the Animals in the Zoo."

Song

Put the Animals in the Zoo

(Sung to: "If You're Happy")

Put the tiger in the zoo, in the zoo.
Put the tiger in the zoo, in the zoo.
Put the tiger in the zoo, and listen to him roar.
Put the tiger in the zoo, in the zoo! ROAR! ROAR!

Repeat with each animal and adapt lyrics as needed.

Instructions for Rabbit Puppets

Materials

several bags of white cotton balls

crayons

glue

pink felt markers

One of each item below per child

white paper lunch sack

white cutout of rabbit head (*pattern below*)

while white pom-pom or large white cotton ball

Prior to the program

Use pink marker to print child's name on the inside lower part of the bag.

Directions

Do this as a group, one step at a time.

1. Give each child a rabbit head to color.

2. Show the children how to glue the rabbit head on the bottom of the bag, so the fold is facing down. When hand is stuck inside the bag, the head will be on top.

3. Give each child a white pom-pom (or large white cotton ball).

4. Show the children how to glue the tail to the back of the rabbit. (This goes on just above the opening to the bag.)

5. Give each child a bunch of cotton balls.

6. Show the children how to glue the cotton balls to both sides of the bag. Let children decide how many cotton balls to put on their bags and where to put them.

open end of bag

rabbit pattern for story bag and puppet

Rabbit Cake
Use two round cakes to make a
rabbit cake. Use the first cake to
create the head. Cut the second
cake as shown to make ears and
bow tie. Decorate with white
frosting as described on p. 42.

rabbit pattern for name tag

Who is this?

Connect the dots to make a picture.
Draw a face on it and color it.

Storybook Birthday Parties

You're Invited!

Mother Goose's
Birthday Party!

Based on the Mother Goose rhymes

Celebrate Mother Goose's Birthday: Program (60 minutes)

Rhyme: "Little Miss Muffet And Little Miss Tucket" Use grasshopper and spider puppets.

Song: "Baa, Baa Black Sheep" As you sing this song, show the children the three bags of black yarn.

Rhyme: "Peter, Peter Pumpkin Eater" (Pattern on p. 49) At the end of the rhyme open the door to reveal Peter and his wife.

Game: London Bridge (Instructions on p. 48)

Rhyme: "Little Bo Peep" Do this as a cut and tell rhyme. (Pattern on p. 49)

Game: Let's Jump Over the Candlestick (Instructions on p. 51)

Rhyme: "Hey Diddle Diddle" Present this as a flannelboard rebus. As you say the rhyme, put up the appropriate picture and let the children tell you the word. Use patterns of your choice.

Game: "The Mouse Ran Up the Clock" (Instructions on p. 52)

Rhyme: "The Old Woman in the Shoe" Say it substituting the words, "She hugged them all tightly and put them to bed."

Game: The Old Woman in the Shoe (Instructions on p. 50)

Rhyme: "Humpty Dumpty" Use a white, raw egg as a prop. Draw Humpty's face on the egg. Have a cookie sheet by your feet. Recite the rhyme, and drop the egg onto the cookie sheet at the appropriate time. Pull out a bottle of glue and ask the children if they can glue Humpty together again. Say, "Of course not! But I'm going to show you a way you can put Humpty together again!"

Project: Humpty Dumpty Puzzle (Instructions on p. 51)

Song: "Mary Had a Little Lamb" (Song on p. 48) Find pictures of a lamb, Mary, school, children and a teacher. Make story cards by gluing each picture on a separate piece of paper. Hold the cards up as you sing the song.

Snacks: Light the candle on the cake and sing "Happy Birthday" to Mother Goose. Blow out the candle and make a wish. Bring each person a piece of cake and a cup of juice.

Story Bags: Give children their story bags as they leave the room.

Planning and Promotion

Advertising Display: Suspend a large goose with Mother Goose riding it from the ceiling. Have a sign underneath with the program and registration information. Have a basket of flyers with the program and registration information for people to take as reminders.

Room Decorations: Try to find Mother Goose-related paper goods (tablecloth, plates, napkins). Decorate the room for a birthday party using banners, streamers and balloons. Have pictures and props from the Mother Goose rhymes.

Puppet: Have a puppet that represents one of the Mother Goose rhymes. The puppet can help with the rhymes.

Guest Character: Have someone dress up and portray Mother Goose. She can help with the program.

Name Tags: Have a variety of Mother Goose shapes such as pumpkin, lamb, star, mitten and heart (patterns on p. 53).

Snacks: Make a "Mary Had a Little Lamb" cake. Use a lamb cake mold or purchase a pre-made lamb cake if you have this program at Easter time. Place one candle in the cake. Have fruit juice for beverage.

Photos: Have an instant camera and take each child's photo arriving at the program. Label photos with the child's first and last name. You will use these to play "The Old Woman in the Shoe Game" on p. 50.

Story Bags: Have a brown lunch sack with a white goose attached. Write the words, **I'VE BEEN TO MOTHER GOOSE'S BIRTHDAY PARTY AT** _____ on the goose. Children can use these to carry home their project, the puzzle on p. 54 and the listing of Mother Goose materials in your library. Party prizes can include: Two patterns for Cut and Tell Nursery Rhymes (p. 52), Miss Muffet Spider Ring, candy hearts, and other Mother Goose items. Label each child's bag with their names before the program. This will allow you to put their projects into the bag later in the program.

Materials and Prep

Mother Goose books

Mother Goose. *Tomie dePaola's Mother Goose.* New York: Putnam, 1985.

Anglund, Joan. *A Mother Goose Book.* New York: Harcourt Brace, 1991.

Tudor, Tasha. *Mother Goose.* New York: Random House, 1989.

Check your library for other books and resources on Mother Goose.

Song

Mary Had a Little Lamb

Mary had a little lamb, a little lamb, a little lamb.
Mary had a little lamb. It's fleece was white as snow.

It followed her to school one, school one day, school one day.
It followed her to school one day, which was against the rule.

It made the children laugh and play, laugh and play, laugh and play.
It made the children laugh and play, to see a lamb in school.

The teacher sent it home again, home again, home again.
The teacher sent it home again, to wait for Mary there.

Instructions for London Bridge Game

Directions

1. Have two parents, other adults or children make the bridge.
2. Have the children form a double file line.
3. Have the children walk hand in hand under the bridge and sing the song.
4. When two children are "caught" take them to the "river bank" where you will let them go. They can sit on the "river bank" and continue to sing along with the others.
5. Keep playing until all children have been "caught and taken to the river bank."

London Bridge is falling down, falling down, falling down.
London Bridge is falling down, my fair children.
Take them to the river bank, river bank, river bank.
Take them to the river bank, and there they can sit down.

Instructions for Peter Peter Pumpkin Eater

Enlarge the pattern below. Cut two identical patterns from orange poster board. Cut windows out of the top pumpkin. Cover the backs of the windows with yellow paper. Cut the door out of the top pumpkin, so it opens and closes.

Glue Peter and his wife in the doorway of the bottom pumpkin. Glue the two pumpkins together. When you open the door, Peter and his wife will greet you.

Peter and his wife

Instructions for Little Bo Peep

Photocopy enlarge the pattern to half sheet size. Then fold the paper in half. Hold the paper so the lines are facing you. Cut out as you recite the rhyme. Leave the top of the sheep's back uncut. When you open the paper, the sheep should stand up.

fold line

Instructions for the Old Woman in the Shoe

Materials

1 large shoe made from brown wrapping paper
It should be large enough so that it is larger than the children. Laminate it or cover it with clear contact paper.

instant camera loaded with film

tape

glue

scissors

shoe box to hold the photos

laminating film and machine or clear contact paper

Prior to the program

1. As each child arrives for the party, quickly take their photo. Tell them you are going to use the photos to play a game later. Put child's name on the back of their photo. Put the photos into a box.

2. Attach the shoe to the wall at child height.

Directions

1. As you sing the song, have two children come up at a time to put their pictures on the shoe. Continue playing until all children have had a turn to put their pictures in the shoe. Parents may come up with children if desired.

2. When finished give the children their photos, or display the finished mural with the rhyme beside it.

Song

Put the Children in the Shoe
(Sung to: "Clementine")

Put the children, put the children, put the children in the shoe.
Put the children, put the children, put the children in the shoe.

Let's put Kelly, let's put Kelly, let's put Kelly in the shoe.
Let's put Ryan, let's put Ryan, let's put Ryan in the shoe.

See the children, see the children, see the children in the shoe.
See the children, see the children, see the children in the shoe.

Instructions for Making the Humpty Dumpty Puzzle

Materials
crayons

paper cutter *(safely out of children's reach)*

contact paper *(optional—If used pre-cut one piece per child. Piece should be large enough to cover both sides of the puzzle.)*

tape

rubber cement

One of each item below per child
picture of Humpty Dumpty

piece of cover stock paper (9" x 11")

 envelope *(labeled with child's name)*

Prior to the program *(Do 24 hours in advance)*
Use rubber cement to attach each puzzle to the cover stock paper.

Directions
Do this as a group, one step at a time.

1. Give each child a puzzle.

2. Let the children use their crayons to color the puzzle.

3. Cover with contact paper if desired.

4. Use the paper cutter to cut puzzle into six pieces. Make one cut lengthwise down the center. Make two cuts across each long piece.

5. Put the puzzle into an envelope, and seal it shut so the pieces don't fall out.

6. Label each envelope with the child's name, and immediately put it into the child's story bag. Tell children they can work their puzzles at home.

Instructions for Let's Jump Over the Candlestick Game

Materials
1 tall size snack food can (potato chips) with plastic lid

1 piece of red construction paper

contact paper (colored and clear)

knife

Prior to the program
1. Cover the can with colored contact paper.

2. Use a knife to make a slit in the top of the plastic lid

3. Cut the red paper to make a flame. Cover it with clear contact paper.

4. Insert the flame into the lid. Tape it on the inside so it stays put.

5. Put the lid on the can.

Directions
1. Have the children sit in a circle. If parents are present, have each parent sit directly behind their own child.

2. Put the candlestick in the center of the circle.

3. Let each child have a turn jumping over the candlestick as you say the rhyme. Substitute each child's name for Jack.

4. Have all of the children say the rhyme together as each child has a turn.

> *Stephanie be nimble,*
> *Stephanie be quick,*
> *Stephanie jump over the candlestick.*

Instructions for Mouse Ran Up the Clock Game

Materials

1 large clock face with movable hands

masking tape

laminating film and machine or clear contact paper

bracket for attaching hands to clock

triangle rhythm instrument (or another instrument you can strike)

Prior to the program

1. Make the clock face and laminate it (or cover with clear contact paper).

2. Make black hands and laminate them (or cover with clear contact paper).

3. Use the bracket to attach the hands to the clock face.

Directions

1. Put the clock face on the floor. Set it to 1:00.

2. Use masking tape to make the lane. The lane will make up the bottom part of the clock with the clock face going on top.

3. Have the children sit in a semicircle at the foot of the clock. If parents are present have them sit directly behind their children.

4. One at a time, each child will have a turn to be the "Mouse" and climb up the clock and run back down. They run like mice on their hands and knees.

5. Lead the children in saying the rhyme as each child pretends to be the mouse. Use the children's names (Mouse Tommy). When you get to the line,

   "The clock struck_____", hit the triangle to indicate the hour.

6. Every time a new child becomes the mouse, move the hands one hour ahead.

7. Kindergartners can each have a turn at striking the hour on the instrument. For younger children who don't yet have the concept of counting, let that child's parent (or another adult) strike the instrument to indicate the hour.

Instructions for Cut & Tell Rhymes

Three Blind Mice

Make copies on a copier. Fold paper in half. The unlined portion should be at the crease. Keep the mouse pattern facing you. Cut on the line as you say the rhyme. Do not cut out the unlined portion of the mouse. Open the paper. The mouse will stand.

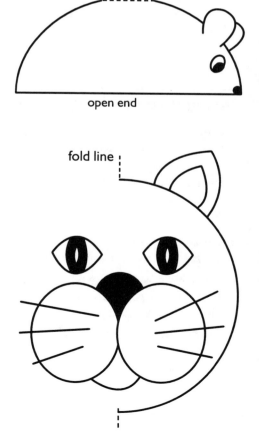

Three blind mice. Three blind mice.
See how they run. See how they run.
They all ran after the farmer's wife.
She cut off their tails with a carving knife.
Did you ever see such a sight in your life.
As three blind mice.

Pussy Cat, Pussy Cat

Copy on copier. Fold paper in half lengthwise. Keep the lines facing you. Cut on the lines as you say the rhyme. Open the paper. You have a cat.

Pussy Cat, Pussy Cat, where have you been?
I've been to London to see the Queen.
Pussy Cat, Pussy Cat what did you do there?
I frightened the little mouse under her chair!

Mother Goose name tag patterns

Whose house is this?

Color the Os, orange; the B, brown; and the Ys, yellow.
What did you make?

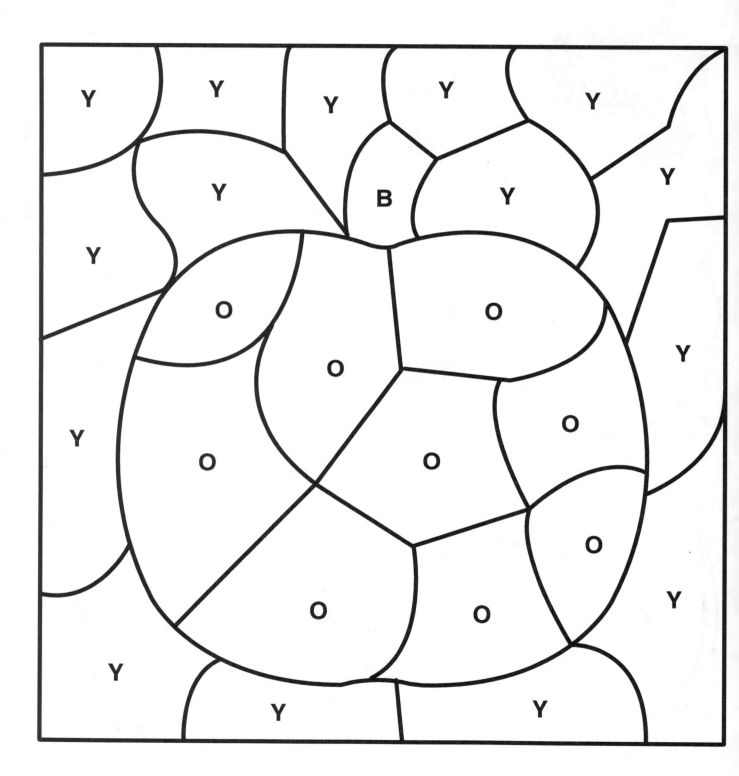

You're Invited!

Spot's Birthday Party!

Based on the books by Eric Hill

Celebrate Spot's 3rd Birthday: Program (45-60 minutes)

Hide Spot in the room before the program begins.

Story: *Where's Spot?* Read this story.

Song: "Where's Spot?" (Instructions on p. 56)

Story: *Spot's Walk in the Woods* Make this into a flannelboard rebus. The children can fill in the words represented by the pictures. Use patterns of your choice.

Game: **Put the Spots on Spot** (Instructions on p. 56)

Story: *Spot Goes to the Circus* Read this story.

Game: **Obedience School** (Instructions on p. 57)

Project: **Dog Magnets** (Instructions on p. 57)

Story: *Spot's Birthday Party* Use props to tell this story to the children.

Snacks: Light the candles on Spot's bone. Sing "Happy Birthday" to Spot. Blow out the candles and make a wish. Pass out cookies and juice.

Story Bags: Give children their story bags as they leave the room. Make sure their magnets are inside the bag.

I've been to Spot's birthday party at:

Planning and Promotion

Advertising Display: Have a dog house with a stuffed Spot peeking out. The program and registration information can be on the dog house. Have a dog bowl next to the dog house. Inside the bowl, put bone-shaped flyers with the program and registration information for people to take home as reminders.

Room Decorations: Create an opening that will fit over the door of the your room. Make it look like the door to a dog house. Decorate the room to look like the inside of Spot's dog house. Try to find dog-themed decorations.

Puppet: Use the Spot the dog toy.

Name Tags: Use the bone-shaped pattern on p. 57.

Snacks: Have bone-shaped cookies for "treats." Serve fruit juice for the beverage. Make a play dough cookie for Spot, insert three candles into it.

Story Bags: Have a brown lunch bag with a cut out of a bone glued to the front. On the bone print, I'VE BEEN TO SPOT'S BIRTHDAY PARTY AT _____ . The children may use their bags to carry home their project, the puzzle on p. 58 and the bone-shaped list of Spot stories available in your library. Party prizes can include: a bone-shaped dog treat for your favorite dog and other dog-related items.

Materials and Prep

Spot books by Eric Hill

Books are listed in series order.

Where's Spot? New York: Putnam, 1980. Spot's mother searches all over until she finds her missing puppy.

Spot's First Walk. New York: Putnam, 1981. Spot finds many surprises when his mother sends him out on a walk.

Spot's Birthday Party. New York: Putnam, 1982. Spot and his friends celebrate his birthday.

Spot's Busy Year. New York: Putnam, 1983. Spot does something special each day of the year.

Spot's First Christmas. New York: Putnam, 1983. Christmas is lots of fun for a little dog.

Spot Tells the Time. New York: Putnam, 1983. Spot learns about telling time.

Spot Goes to School. New York: Putnam, 1984. Spot has fun learning things at school.

Spot at Home. New York: Putnam, 1985. Spot and his friends have fun playing together.

Spot at the Fair. New York: Putnam, 1985. Spot and his friends have fun at the amusement park.

Spot Goes to the Beach. New York: Putnam, 1985. Spot and his family have fun at the beach.

Spot's First Words. New York: Putnam, 1986. Spot learns many new words.

Spot Goes to the Circus. New York: Putnam, 1986. Spot goes to the circus, where he learns a new trick.

Spot's Big Book of Words. New York: Putnam, 1988. Spot learns many new words.

Spot's First Easter. New York: Putnam, 1988. Spot looks for hidden eggs.

Spot Looks at Opposites. New York: Putnam, 1989. Spot learns about empty and full, fast and slow & other opposites.

Spot Looks at Weather. New York: Putnam, 1989. Spot learns about all kinds of weather.

Spot's Baby Sister. New York: Putnam, 1989. Spot has a new baby sister.

Spot's Big Book of Colors. New York: Putnam, 1989. Spot learns about colors.

Spot Sleeps Over. New York: Putnam, 1990. Spot forgets something he needs for the sleepover at Steve's house.

Spot Goes to the Park. New York: Putnam, 1991. Spot has lots of fun playing in the park.

Spot in the Garden. New York: Putnam, 1991. Spot has adventures playing in the garden.

Spot's Toy Box. New York: Putnam, 1991. Spot has great toys in his toy box.

Spot's Walk in the Woods. New York: Putnam, 1993. Spot and his classmates go on a field trip, where they see many interesting things.

Spot Bakes a Cake. New York: Putnam, 1994. Spot bakes a cake for his dad's birthday.

Spot's Magical Christmas. New York: Putnam, 1995. Spot has an exciting Christmas celebration.

Song

Where Is Spot?
(Sung to: "Frere Jacques")
Where is Spot?
Where is Spot?

He is hiding!
He is hiding!

Let's try and find him!
Let's try and find him!

Where is he?
Where is he?

Encourage children to suggest places where Spot may be hiding. When you find him say, "Spot! Here you are! I'm so glad we found you. We're having your birthday party today." Spot can respond.

Instructions for Put the Spots on Spot Game

Materials
1 very large picture of Spot   *Tape the piece of paper to the wall. With an overhead projector, enlarge Spot. Trace it and cut it out. Don't draw the spots on Spot.*

1 brown construction-paper spot per child

laminating film and machine or clear contact paper

Prior to the program
1. Color or paint Spot yellowish brown. Let dry 24 hrs.
2. Laminate Spot or cover him with clear contact.
3. Put Spot on the wall with his feet next to the floor.
4. Put the brown spots into a bag.

Directions
1. Have the children sit on the floor.
2. Have children come up one at a time.
3. Let child pull a spot from the bag and place on Spot.
4. Sing the Spots on Spot song while child chooses where to put his or her spot.

Put the Spots on Spot
(Sung to: "The Farmer in the Dell")
Put the spots on Spot, put the spots on Spot.
Look, look, look at us, we put the spots on Spot.

Instructions for Obedience School

Explain that puppies have to go to Obedience School. They learn how to behave and do tricks. "Today, all of you can pretend to be puppies at Obedience School."

Directions

1. Have the "puppies" (children) form a large circle. Their "masters" (parents) will stand behind their children.

2. Now have the "puppies" turn and face their "masters."

3. Stand in the center of the circle and give obedience commands: Sit, beg, shake, speak, roll over etc.

4. When the "puppies" perform correctly, their "masters" can pat them on the head and say, "Good Boy/Girl."

Note: If parents are not present, keep the children facing the inside of the circle. Give out the commands. When the "puppies" perform correctly, say "Good Dogs!"

Instructions for Dog Magnets

Materials

fabric glue

markers

glue gun and glue *(for adult use only)*

white small self-stick labels

One of each item below per child

1 felt Spot *(Use a light gold color)*

3 brown felt spots

1 set of movable eyes *(Brown felt eyes can be substituted.)*

1 small, black pom-pom for the nose *(Black felt circle can be substituted.)*

2 brown felt ears

1 magnet *(It should be long enough to go almost all the way across the back of Spot.)*

Prior to the program

1. Use a glue gun to attach the magnets to the Spot cutouts. Let dry for 24 hours.

2. Print each child's first and last name on a label and make sure children's names are on the story bags.

Directions

Do this as a group, one step at a time.

1. Give each child a Spot.

2. Give each child two eyes and show them how to glue them on Spot. Put one on each side.

3. Give each child a nose and glue these on Spot.

4. Give each child two ears and glue the ears on Spot.

5. Give each child three spots to glue on Spot.

6. Attach each child's name label to their dog and place in the story bags. Tell children Spot is napping.

bone pattern for name tag and story bag

Spot pattern for magnet

Can you find the missing bones?

Spot has buried five bones in the yard. He can't remember where they are. Can you help Spot find his bones? Circle the bones you find. Then color the picture.

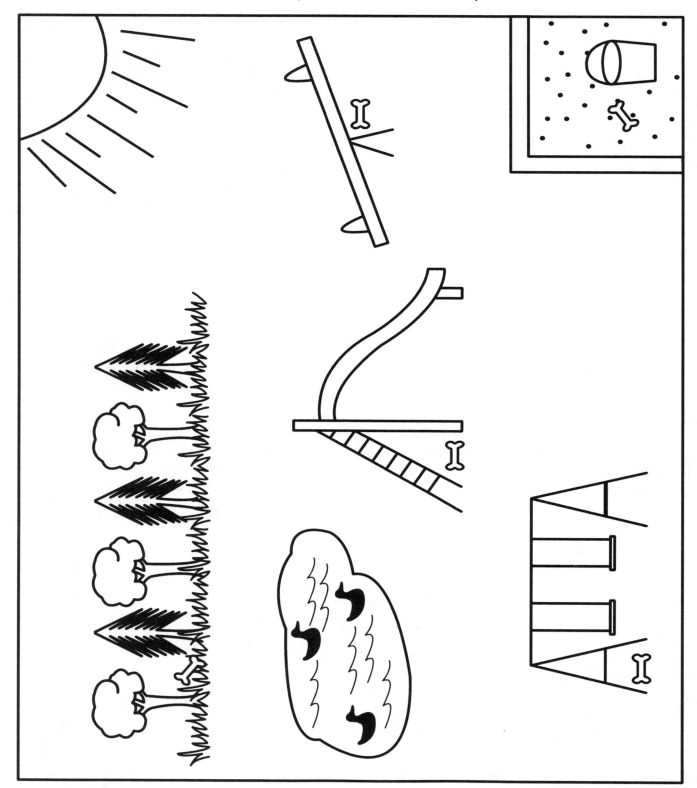

Parties for Kindergarten – 2nd Grade

The parties in this section are for children in kindergarten through 2nd grade. You can accommodate between twenty and thirty children at these programs. When doing these programs in a public library, bookstore or park district setting it is recommended that you suggest parents remain in the building during the program. You need to be able to locate a parent quickly should a problem or emergency arise.

Parties need at least two staff members to present the program. A couple of the parties include treasure hunts which need one person to assist each group of children. "Guest Characters" are an important part of some parties. When sharing these programs in a school setting, ask your room parents to help. Libraries, park districts and bookstores can ask volunteers to assist. You can also ask parents of children attending the program to assist. Be sure to meet with your volunteers prior to each program, so that they know what is expected of them.

Parties include stories, games, activities, music and projects. Of course birthday refreshments are included. Let parents know that food will be served. Be willing to accommodate special diets children are on by offering an alternative snack. In some cases it may be best if the child's parent or guardian supplies a snack.

When scheduling parties in libraries, park districts and bookstores, try to offer each program several times. Plan parties for after school, evenings and weekends. School holidays also provide good opportunities for such programs. This allows you to accommodate the various schedules people have.

Try to follow the format for each program. Programs have been carefully designed to appeal to the development of children in this age group. You will note that stories are usually followed by a related activity. Having activities related to the story, helps to reinforce it and adds to the children's enjoyment of it.

The objectives for these parties include:
*   Introduce the children to book characters
*   Encourage a love of and appreciation of literature
*   Develop reading and listening skills
*   Enhance creativity (art projects)
*   Develop social skills in a group situation (taking turns)
*   Develop problem solving skills

You're Invited!

Amelia Bedelia's Birthday Party!

Based on the books by Peggy Parish and Herman Parish

Celebrate Amelia's 20th Birthday: Program (60-90 minutes)

Story: **Amelia Bedelia** Right after you finish reading this story, have a knock on the door. It will be Amelia Bedelia coming to a "birthday party." However she does not know that it is a "surprise party" for her. She should act mixed-up throughout the program.

Game: **Pin the What on What?** (Instructions on p. 62)

Story: **Teach Us, Amelia Bedelia** Have Amelia Bedelia tell this story to the children.

Project: **Sponge Paintings** Let Amelia Bedelia teach this. (Instructions on p. 62)

Booktalks: Choose several Amelia Bedelia books. Tell about one or two incidents in each, but do not divulge the outcome. Encourage the children to check these out if they want to know what happened. Amelia Bedelia can tell about some of the books.

Story: **Amelia Bedelia's Family Album** Do this in tandem with Amelia Bedelia. Prior to the program, make a family album of Amelia Bedelia' family. She can share this with the children as the two of you tell the story.

Project: **Make a Family Album** (Instructions on p. 63)

Story: **Good Driving, Amelia Bedelia** Read this story about Amelia's birthday.

Snacks: Light the candles on the cake. Sing "Happy Birthday" to Amelia Bedelia. Now she will know that this is her "surprise party." Bring each child a piece of cake and a cup of juice.

Story Bags: Give children their story bags as they leave. Be sure they have their sponge paintings and family albums to take home.

I've been to Amelia Bedelia's birthday party at:

Planning and Promotion

Advertising Display: Have a cutout of Amelia Bedelia attached to a sign with the program and registration information. Make the sign "mixed-up." Some of the information can be written upside down, sideways, etc. Provide flyers for people to take home.

Room Decorations: Decorate the room with crazy, mixed-up decorations. (Have a pan of bread hanging from the lights and other silly things from the stories.) Choose a colorful, patterned tablecloth. Provide paper plates, cups and napkins in a variety of crazy colors and patterns.

Guest Character: Have someone on staff dress up and portray Amelia Bedelia. She can help with the program.

Planning and Promotion

name Tags: Use any birthday name tag. The sillier the better. Print the child's last name first and their first name last. Use a variety of marker colors and letter styles.

Photos: Have an instant camera loaded with film. Take a photo of each child arriving for the party. Print the child's name on the back of their photo. You will use this later on.

Snacks: Make a mixed-up birthday cake and juice. Make four small pans of cake, each one a different flavor (yellow, chocolate, strawberry, white) You can add colored sprinkles to the yellow or white cake batter, and M & M's to the chocolate and strawberry batter if desired. Join the cakes together to make one large cake. Frost with white frosting and print **HAPPY BIRTHDAY, AMELIA BEDELIA** across the top. Have fun with the lettering. Print some of the letters upside down, backwards. Put the candles so they are coming out the sides of the cake.

Story Bags: Provide white lunch sacks that say, **I'VE BEEN TO AMELIA BEDELIA'S BIRTHDAY PARTY AT** _____. The children can use the bag to carry home their family album. Party prizes can include: crazy pencils, erasers, etc. Be sure to give each child the puzzle on p.64 and a list of Amelia Bedelia materials your library owns.

Materials

Amelia Bedelia books

Books are listed in series order. Amelia Bedelia books were written by Peggy Parish through 1988, the last two titles were written by her nephew, Herman Parish.

Amelia Bedelia. New York: HarperCollins, 1963, 1991. Amelia Bedelia gets a job working for the Rogers family. She follows the directions Mrs. Rogers gives her, but everything gets mixed up.

Thank You, Amelia Bedelia. New York: HarperCollins, 1964, 1992. Amelia helps get ready for company. What a disaster!

Amelia Bedelia and the Surprise Shower. New York: Harper & Row, 1966. Amelia Bedelia and her Cousin Alcolu help Mrs. Rogers give Miss Alma a surprise wedding shower.

Come Back, Amelia Bedelia. New York: HarperCollins, 1971. Mrs. Rogers is so frustrated with Amelia Bedelia that she fires her.

Play Ball, Amelia Bedelia. New York: HarperCollins, 1972. Amelia Bedelia is filling in for a sick baseball player. What a game!

Good Work, Amelia Bedelia. New York: Greenwillow, 1976. Amelia Bedelia pots the plants, patches the screen door and makes a sponge cake. What a day!

Teach Us, Amelia Bedelia. New York: Greenwillow, 1977. Amelia Bedelia is the substitute teacher. She and the kids have a great day!

Amelia Bedelia Helps Out. New York: Greenwillow, 1979. Amelia Bedelia spends the day working in the garden.

Amelia Bedelia and the Baby. New York: Greenwillow, 1981. Amelia Bedelia spends an exhausting day babysitting.

Amelia Bedelia Goes Camping. New York: Greenwillow, 1985. What fun Amelia Bedelia has when she goes camping with the Rogers family.

Merry Christmas, Amelia Bedelia. New York: Greenwillow, 1986. Amelia Bedelia helps Mrs. Rogers prepare for Christmas.

Amelia Bedelia's Family Album. New York: Greenwillow, 1988. Amelia Bedelia shows Mr. and Mrs. Rogers her family album.

Good Driving, Amelia Bedelia. New York: Greenwillow, 1995. Amelia Bedelia celebrates her birthday with a drive in the country and a party.

Bravo, Amelia Bedelia. New York: Greenwillow, 1997. Amelia causes all sorts of trouble at the school concert.

Instructions for Pin the What on What? Game

Materials

large mural with drawings of animals (elephant, giraffe, leopard, peacock, etc.) *Draw just the body (omit the elephant's trunk, the giraffe's neck, the leopard's spots, the peacock's tail.) and color it in. Use white paper that comes on a roll.*

cutouts of animal body parts (elephant trunk, giraffe neck, leopard spots, peacock tail, etc.) *There should be one per child.*

tape

large box

blindfold

Prior to the program

1. If desired, laminate the mural and body parts. This allows you to reuse the mural for several programs without worrying about tears. You can also use clear contact paper.

2. Put the body parts into a large box.

Directions

1. Have children come up one at a time.

2. Blindfold the child.

3. Hold the box up over the child's head. Let the child remove a body part from the box.

4. Point the child in the direction of the mural and let them try to put their body part on the right animal. You'll have an interesting mural when finished.

5. Display the mural for others to enjoy.

Instructions for Sponge Painting

Let Amelia Bedelia lead this.

Materials

pie tins

tempera paints in a variety of colors

paint brushes

1 large meat tray per child

sponge cutouts *(available from craft stores/teacher stores)* Have at least one per child.

1 large kitchen sponge

1 piece of white, heavy duty construction paper per child (10" x 12")

markers

Prior to the program

Mix the tempera paints so they are reasonably thick. Put each color into a separate pie tin.

Directions

Do this as a group, one step at a time.

1. Have Amelia Bedelia say, "We are supposed to make sponge paintings. I've never made a sponge painting, but if that's what they want us to do, that's what we are going to do."

   Amelia says, "In a couple of minutes, I will give each of you a sponge to paint.

   This is what you do. Take your brush, dip it into the paint and paint a picture on your sponge. I think I'll paint a tree on mine." She starts to paint a tree.

2. The children will have a variety of reactions. Some will go along with it, while others will question if this is what they are supposed to do.

3. You can ask the children, "Have any of you ever done sponge paintings before?"

   (Yes!) "How did you do them?" (Let the children tell you and Amelia Bedelia how to make sponge paintings.)

4. Now, pass out the paper, and give each child a sponge shape.

5. Help the children use markers to print their names on their papers.

6. Show Amelia and the children how to dip the sponge into the paint and dab it onto the paper, leaving a print. Remind the children not to move the sponge around on the paper. Touch it to the paper and pull it right up.

7. Follow the rule of one color per sponge.

8. .Let the paintings dry. Children may take these home.

   Hint: Amelia needs to stay "in character." She should act surprised when she learns how to sponge paint.

Instructions for Make a Family Album

Materials

3-hole paper punch

crayons

glue

Items below are required for each child

individual photo of each child. *(See Photos, p. 61.)*

1 pencil

2 pieces of cover stock paper (10" x 12")

3 brackets *(Use bracket rather than staples. That allows them to add to their books.)*

Prior to the program

1. Create a simple cover as shown leaving a space for children to print their names.

2. Make six copies per child of the album page below.

Child's Name
_____

Family Album

Directions

Do this as a group, one step at a time.

1. Give each child a front cover. Let them use the crayons to print their names in the space provided. They can decorate it.

2. Give each child his/her own photo. Show them how to glue it in the space provided on the album page.

3. Give each child an album page. Help them fill it out with information about themselves.

4. Give each child five more copies of album page. Tell them their parents can bring them to the library to make additional copies of this page if they need them.

5. Tell children they can fill out a page for each family member. They will do this at home with the help of their families.

6. Give each child a back cover. Three hole punch each child's album. Fasten it together with brackets.

7. If desired, you can encourage the children to return to the library with their completed family albums. Give them a prize when they do (bookmark).

album page

> **All about** _____ _____   PHOTO
>
> **Birthdate:** _____   **Place of birth:** _____
>
> **Eye color:** _____   **Hair color:** _____
>
> **Favorite color:** _____   **Favorite animal:** _____
>
> **Favorite foods:** _____
>
> **Favorite book:** _____
>
> **Favorite TV show:** _____
>
> **Favorite song:** _____
>
> **Best friends:** _____
>
> **Hobbies:** _____
>
> **Tell some other interesting things about yourself (or this person.)**
>
> _____
>
> _____
>
> _____
>
> _____

A Secret Message

The letters from each type of shape must be unscrambled to find the message. To help decode the message, color the shapes as follows: circles – blue, squares – yellow, stars – purple, rectangles – orange, triangles – green. Then unscramble to get the words of the message. The shapes at the bottom of the page tell you where to print each word.

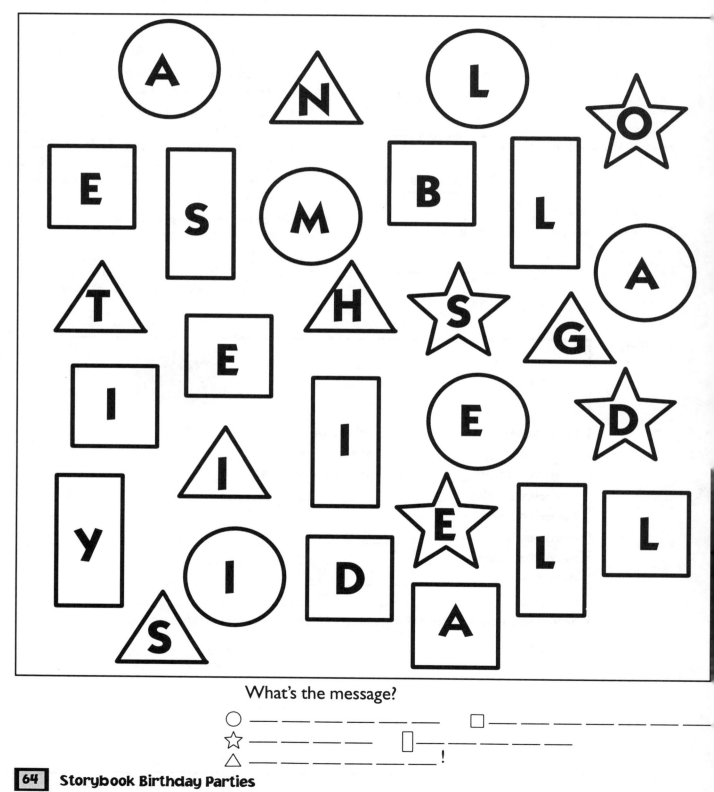

What's the message?

○ —— —— —— —— —— —— —— ——   ☐ —— —— —— ——
☆ —— —— —— —— —— ——   ▯ —— —— —— ——
△ —— —— —— —— —— —— —— !

You're Invited!

Jimmy's Birthday Party!

Based on the books by Trinka Hakes Noble

Celebrate Jimmy's 8th Birthday: Program (60-90 minutes)

Story: *The Day Jimmy's Boa Ate the Wash* Read this story.

Project: **Create a Boa Constrictor** (Instructions on p. 66)

Story: *Jimmy's Boa Bounces Back* Read this story.

Activity: **Book Boa** (Instructions on p. 67)

Story: *Jimmy's Boa and the Big Splash Birthday Bash* Read this story.

Game: **Let's Go Fishing** (Instructions on p. 67)

Snacks: Light the candles on the cake, and sing "Happy Birthday" to Jimmy. Blow out the candles and make a wish. Give each child a piece of cake and a cup of juice.

Story Bags: Give children their story bags as they leave the room.

Planning and Promotion

Advertising Display: Use poster board to create a large goldfish bowl. Have fish swimming in it. Print the program and registration information on the fish. Provide fish-shaped flyers with the program and registration information on them for people to take as reminders.

Room Decorations: Use a fish theme to decorate the room. Have fish hanging from the ceiling and swimming on the walls. Use a tablecloth, plates, napkins and cups with a fish theme or use fish stickers on plain cups, tablecloth and plates.

Puppet: Try to find snake, fish, whale and octopus puppets or stuffed toys.

Name Tags: Use the snake pattern on p. 66.

Snacks: Have a white cake decorated with blue frosting. Decorate it with fish. Print "Happy Birthday, Jimmy" on the cake. Serve blue punch as the beverage.

Story Bags: Have a white lunch sack with a fish attached. Print, **I'VE BEEN TO JIMMY'S BIRTHDAY PARTY AT** _____. on the tag. The children can use these to carry home the prize they catch "fishing" on p. 67 and the puzzle on p. 68. Use other inexpensive fish- or boa constrictor-related items you choose for party prizes if desired.

Materials and Prep

Jimmy books by Trinka Hakes Noble

Books are listing in series order.

The Day Jimmy's Boa Ate the Wash. New York: Dial Books for Young Readers, 1980. Jimmy's class has quite an exciting field trip to the farm. His boa causes all sorts of trouble.

Jimmy's Boa Bounces Back. New York: Dial Books for Young Readers, 1984. Jimmy's boa causes a lot of trouble at the garden club meeting.

Jimmy's Boa and the Big Splash Birthday Bash. New York: Dial Books for Young Readers, 1989. Jimmy's birthday party is filled with excitement when his boa accompanies him and his party guests to the aquarium.

Instructions for Boa Constrictor

Materials
scissors

paper punch

crayons

One of each item below per child
1 boa reproduced on card stock *(pattern below)*

1 6" piece of yarn

2 small movable eyes *(optional)*

Directions
1. Give each child a boa circle and crayons.
2. Tell the children to color their circle so that both sides are covered with crayon. They can choose how to color it.
3. Show them how to cut out the circle so it becomes a boa.
4. Have the children color eyes on the snake. (Optional: Give each child two eyes. Show children how to glue these to the boa's head.)
5. Punch a hole in the top of the boa's head.
6. String the yarn through so it can be hung.
7. Display these or let the children take them home.

Patterns

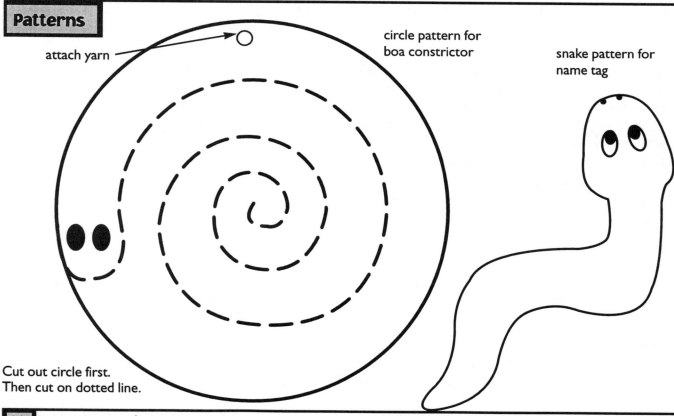

attach yarn

circle pattern for boa constrictor

snake pattern for name tag

Cut out circle first.
Then cut on dotted line.

Instructions for Book Boa

Materials:
1 4" book boa circle per child   *Use a variety of colors.*

pencils

boa head that you create

Directions

1. Give each child a circle and a pencil.

2. Tell them to fill out the circle with their name and grade.

3. Have them print the title of their favorite book in the space provided. (Assist with printing as needed.)

4. Tape these together to form a long book boa.

5. Tell the children that every time they read a book at home or have a book read to them, they can add another segment to the book boa.

6. See how far your snake will reach by a certain date.

Note: *This is a good way to begin a reading program for children this age. Try to involve parents by encouraging them read to their children (or listen to their children read) at home.*

Your Name: _____

Grade: _____

Book Title: _____

The best part was _____

_____

_____.

book boa pattern

Instructions for Let's Go Fishing

Materials

1 child's swimming pool

magnet strips

paper clips

fish pattern (1 fish per child)

prizes (fish stickers)

dowel rod with a piece of rope attached
    Attach a magnet to the end of the rope.

Directions

1. Attach paper clips to the fish.

2. Put the fish into the pool.

3. Let each child have a turn to fish.

4. As soon as they catch a fish, award children with a fish sticker.

    Hints: *Play some lively birthday party music while the children are fishing.*

    Make four fishing rods and let four children fish at one time.

fish pattern for story bag and
Let's Go Fishing

Look Carefully

Look carefully and see if you can find: a fish, an octopus, a shark, a seal, and a boa constrictor. When you find them, color them.

You're Invited!

Pinkerton's Birthday Party!

Based on the books by Steven Kellogg

Celebrate Pinkerton's 7th Birthday: Program (60-90 minutes)

Story: *Pinkerton, Behave!* Read this story.

Activity: **Measure Up** (Instructions on p. 71)

Story: *Prehistoric Pinkerton* Let the dog puppet help with this story.

Activity: **Tell Us About Pinkerton** (Instructions on p. 70)

Song: **"Aren't We Good Dogs?"** (Song on p. 70)

Project: **Make a Birthday Card for Pinkerton** (Instructions on p. 72)

Game: **Give a Bone to Pinkerton** (Instructions on p. 72)

Booktalks: Choose other Pinkerton stories to highlight. Tell the story up to the climax, but don't reveal the ending. Encourage the children to read the books to find out how they end.

Project: **Make a Dog Puppet** (Instructions on p. 71)

Snacks: Light the candles on Pinkerton's bone cookie. Sing "Happy Birthday" to Pinkerton. Blow out the candles and make a wish. Bring each child one bone cookie and a cup of juice.

Story Bags: Give children their story bags as they leave. Make sure the puppet each child made is inside the bag.

Planning and Promotion

Advertising Display: Have a large dog made from poster board. He can be holding a large sign that has the program and registration information. Provide flyers with the program and registration information for people to take.

Room Decorations: Create an original large dog from cardboard. It should go from floor to ceiling. Cut it out and laminate it. Add eyes, nose, mouth, ears and collar. Put the dog on the wall with its feet at the floor. Put a measuring tape alongside the whole height of the dog (See p. 71 for instructions.). Have streamers and balloons. Use the computer to create a **HAPPY BIRTHDAY, PINKERTON** banner to hang in the area.

Puppet: Use a large dog puppet or stuffed toy.

Name Tags: Use the dog pattern on p. 72.

Snacks: Have bone-shaped sugar cookies. Bone cookie cutters can be found in pet stores and home stores. Make one larger bone out of brown play dough. Stick seven candles into it. Serve cranberry juice for the beverage.

Story Bags: Use white lunch sacks. Attach a dog cut out. Use pattern on p. 72. Print, **I'VE BEEN TO PINKERTON'S BIRTHDAY PARTY AT** _____ . Children can use their bags to carry home the dog puppet, the puzzle on p. 73 and a bone-shaped listing of the Pinkerton materials in your library. Party prizes can include: a bone-shaped dog treat for your favorite dog, dog related items (erasers, pencils, dog tag, stickers, etc.)

Pinkerton books by Steven Kellogg

Books are listed in series order.

Pinkerton, Behave! New York: Dial Books for Young Readers, 1979. Pinkerton has to learn how to behave. What a challenge!

A Rose for Pinkerton. New York: Dial Books for Young Readers, 1981. Pinkerton has a new companion. She is a kitten named Rose.

Tallyho, Pinkerton! New York: Dial Books for Young Readers, 1982. Pinkerton and Rose cause all sorts of trouble on a trip to the woods.

Prehistoric Pinkerton. New York: Dial Books for Young Readers, 1987. Pinkerton goes on a field trip where he is introduced to the dinosaurs.

Song

Aren't We Good Dogs?
(Sung to: "Mary Had a Little Lamb")

We are going to do dog tricks, do dog tricks, do dog tricks.
We are going to do dog tricks,
Aren't we good dogs?

Watch us as we say hello, say hello, say hello.
[Dogs wave paws]
Watch us as we say hello,
Aren't we good dogs?

Watch us as we sit and beg, sit and beg, sit and beg
[Dogs sit and beg]
Watch us as we sit and beg.
Aren't we good dogs?

Watch us as we roll right over, roll right over, roll right over
[Dogs roll over]
Watch us as we roll right over.
Aren't we good dogs?

Listen as we speak to you, speak to you, speak to you.
[Dogs bark]
Listen as we speak to you.
Aren't we good dogs?

Watch us as we sit right down, sit right down, sit right down
[Dogs sit down.]
Watch us as we sit right down.
Aren't we good dogs?

Instructions for Tell Us About Pinkerton

Materials
chalk board or an easel with a pad of paper
chalk or black marker

Prior to the program
Print Pinkerton's name vertically on the writing surface

Directions
1. Tell the children that an adjective is a word that describes someone. Think of adjectives that describe people you know (tall, funny, happy, etc.)

2. Tell the children that we are going to think of adjectives about Pinkerton. But each adjective must begin with a letter of Pinkerton's name.

3. Remind the children that the adjectives describe or tell us about Pinkerton.

Here are a couple of ideas to get you started.

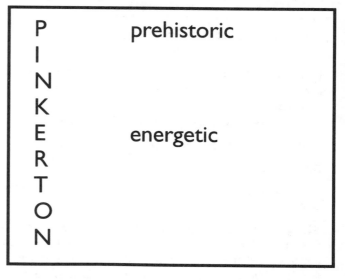

Instructions for Making Dog Puppet

Materials
black marker for writing names on paint sticks

One of each item below per child
1 cardboard dog
1 set of movable eyes
1 black crayon
1 paint stick

Directions
Do this together as a group, one step at a time.

1. Give each child a cardboard dog.

2. Give each child a set of movable eyes. Show them how to glue the eyes to front of the dog's face.

3. Give each child a black crayon. Let them draw a nose, and mouth on the front. Have them use any color to add a collar.

4. Give each child a paint stick. Have children print their names on their paint sticks. Print it toward the bottom of the stick.

5. Show children how to glue the dog to the paint stick.

6. Tell the children to name give a name to their dog.

7. Let puppet dry flat. Tell the children to wait until the next day to use the puppet so that it can dry.

8. Put the puppets in the story bags as they leave.

Instructions for Measure Up

Materials
dog pattern enlarged for the wall
slips of paper
marker
tape measure

Directions
1. One at a time, have each child come and stand along side the tape measure.

2. Print the child's name on the slip of paper.

3. Measure the child.

4. Note the child's height on the slip of paper.

5. Tape it to the proper spot.

6. See how the children "measure up" to your dog.

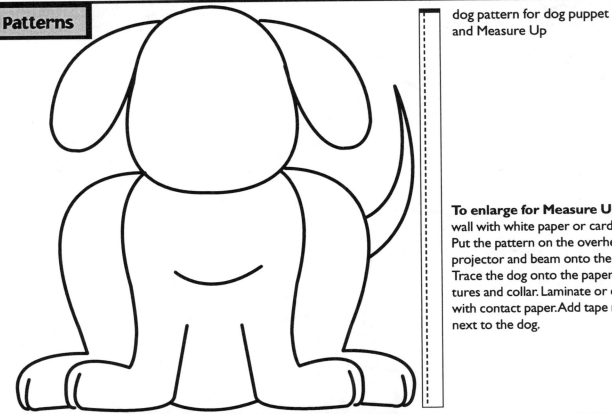

dog pattern for dog puppet and Measure Up

To enlarge for Measure Up: Cover wall with white paper or cardboard. Put the pattern on the overhead projector and beam onto the wall. Trace the dog onto the paper. Add features and collar. Laminate or cover with contact paper. Add tape measure next to the dog.

Instructions for Make a Birthday Card

Materials
crayons
hole punch
paper clips

One of each item below per child
2 sheets of cover stock paper (10" x 12") *Use a variety of colors. Cut these into two identical dogs (pattern below), and paper clip them together.*
1 sheet of white paper *Cut this into a dog shape. Use copier to reduce the pattern.*
yarn cut into two 12" pieces

Prior to the program
Punch two holes in the top of the dogs.

Directions
Do this together as a group, one step at a time.

1. Give each child a white dog.

2. Allow children to decorate the dogs and write birthday greetings to Pinkerton. Encourage them to use both sides of the white paper. Have them sign their names. Help those children who need assistance.

3. Give each child two colored dogs.

4. Have children draw a face on one side of each dog. It helps to keep the two dogs paper clipped together.

5. Put the white dogs between the two colored dogs.

6. Attach all three sheets with red yarn .

7. Send the cards to Steven Kellogg with a letter from you telling about the program. If he replies, include his letter on a poster with the photos you took.

Alternatives: Make a group card. Put all of the children's birthday greetings inside one colored dog card. Display the birthday cards for all to enjoy.

Instructions for Give a Bone to Pinkerton

Materials
1 very large, deep dog dish
1 box of dog bone cookies (1 bone per child)
masking tape

Prior to the program
Put a masking tape line on the floor.

Directions
1. Put the dish on the floor.

2. Have each child take a turn standing behind the line and tossing a bone into the dog dish.

Hint: Vary the distance between the dish and the line depending upon the age and ability of the children.

Patterns

punch holes to tie yarn for birthday card

dog pattern for name tags and birthday cards (Enlarge or reduce as needed.)

Where are they?

This dog has lost several things. Can you help him find his bone,
ball, egg, collar and bowl? Color each item you find.

You're Invited!

Arthur's Birthday Party!

Based on the books by Lillian Hoban

Celebrate Arthur's 6th Birthday: Program (60-90 minutes)

Story: *Arthur's Honey Bear* Read this story.

Song: "Silly, Funny Monkey" (Song on p. 75)

Story: *Arthur's Prize Reader* Read this story.

Game: The Alphabet Game (Instructions on p. 76)

Story: *Arthur's Camp Out* Read this story.

Project: Make Newspaper Hats (Instructions on p. 76)

Booktalks: Highlight the Arthur Monkey books not used in the program. Tell the story up to the climax, but do not supply the ending. Encourage the children to read the book to find out how the story ends.

Snacks: Light the candles on the cake. Sing "Happy Birthday" to Arthur Monkey. Blow out the candles and make a wish. Bring each child a piece of cake and a cup of juice.

Story Bags: Give children their story bags as they leave. Make sure their prizes and hats are in the bag.

Planning and Promotion

Advertising Display: Have an Arthur Monkey puppet or stuffed toy riding a bike. He can be carrying a sign that has the program and registration information. Include monkey-shaped flyers with the program and registration information for people to take as reminders.

Room Decorations: Decorate for a birthday party using colorful balloons. **HAPPY BIRTHDAY, ARTHUR MONKEY** banners, streamers, etc. Try to find a paper tablecloth, plates, cups and napkins with a monkey theme.

Puppet: Use a monkey puppet. He can help with the program.

Name Tags: Use the monkey pattern on p. 76.

Snacks: Have a birthday cake and juice. Draw a picture of a monkey on the cake. Write Happy Birthday Arthur on the cake. Put six candles in the cake.

Story Bags: Have white bags with a brown monkey that says: **I'VE BEEN TO ARTHUR MONKEY'S BIRTHDAY PARTY AT** _____ . The pattern is on p. 76. The children can carry home their projects, the puzzle on p. 77 and a monkey-shaped list of the Arthur Monkey materials in your library in the bag. Party prizes can include: monkey stickers and monkey-related items (banana magnet, etc.).

Materials and Prep

Arthur books by Lillian Hoban

Books are listed in series order.

Arthur's Christmas Cookies. New York: HarperCollins, 1972. Arthur tries to make Christmas cookies for his friends, but they don't turn out right. They taste funny and they are very hard.

Arthur's Honey Bear. New York: Harper & Row, 1972. Arthur is sorry he has sold Honey Bear at a tag sale.

Arthur's Pen Pal. New York: HarperTrophy, 1976. Arthur decides it might be more fun to have a brother rather than a sister.

Arthur's Prize Reader. New York: Harper & Row, 1978. Violet proves to Arthur that she really can read.

Arthur's Funny Money. New York: Harper & Row, 1981. Arthur and Lillian try to earn money washing bikes.

Arthur's Halloween Costume. New York: HarperCollins, 1984. Arthur has the most unusual costume ever. What is it?

Arthur's Loose Tooth. New York: Harper & Row, 1985. Arthur is afraid of blood, so he doesn't want to lose his tooth.

Arthur's Great Valentine. New York: HarperCollins, 1989. Arthur decides he isn't going to make any Valentines this year.

Arthur's Camp Out. New York: HarperCollins, 1993. The girls come to Arthur's rescue when everything goes wrong on the camp out.

Arthur's Back to School Day. New York: HarperCollins, 1996. Arthur ends up with quite a surprise when he takes the wrong lunch to school.

Song

Silly, Funny Monkey

(Sung to: "Skip to My Lou")
Do the motions with the children as you sing

Look at that silly, funny monkey!
Look at that silly, funny monkey!
Look at that silly, funny monkey!
Look at what he does!

He taps his toes and scratches his nose!
He taps his toes and scratches his nose!
He taps his toes and scratches his nose!
Look at what he does!

He jumps up high and claps his hands!
He jumps up high and claps his hands!
He jumps up high and claps his hands!
Look at what he does!

He turns in a circle and waves his arms!
He turns in a circle and waves his arms!
He turns in a circle and waves his arms!
Look at what he does!

Do this part very fast

He taps his toes and scratches his head!
He jumps up high and claps his hands!
He turns in a circle and waves his arms!
Look at what he does!

He turns, waves, claps, taps, and scratches!
He turns, waves, claps, taps, and scratches!
He turns, waves, claps, taps, and scratches!
Look at what he does!

He sits back down and gets real quiet.
He sits back down and gets real quiet.
He sits back down and gets real quiet.
He doesn't make a sound!

Instructions for Alphabet Game

Materials

I set of laminated upper case alphabet cards. *Use letter stencils to trace the letters. Color them in with bright, easy-to-read colors (red, green, blue, purple—avoid yellow)*

I set of laminated lower case alphabet cards *Color code them to the upper case letters.*

letter stencils

bright colored markers

laminating film and machine or clear contact paper

pictures that represent each letter *(A=apple, B=bear)*

Prior to the program

I. Put the upper case alphabet on the wall at child height in alphabetical order. Put a dividing space between M and N so there thirteen letters on each side.

2. Put lower case letters A–M in one pile and their corresponding pictures in the same pile. Mix them up.

3. Put the lower case letters N–Z and their corresponding pictures into a second pile. Scramble them.

Directions

I. Divide children into two teams.

2. At your signal, the first child in each team pulls out a card. It might be a letter or a picture. They must quickly find the proper upper case card and match it. Have them set the card on the floor directly under the upper case letter.

3. When both children have matched their cards, have them go to the end of the line.

4. Repeat until all children have had a turn.

5. Give each child an alphabet bookmark or something else related to the alphabet for their story bags.

Hints: Adapt this to the age and ability of the children you work with. You might want to just match pictures to letters or lower case to upper case letters. Help children as needed.

This isn't a race to see who wins. It's to help children recognize letters and learn letter sounds. Tell the children this is a game Arthur might play in school.

Instructions for Newspaper Hats

Materials

newspapers

markers

feathers (one per child)

glitter

glue

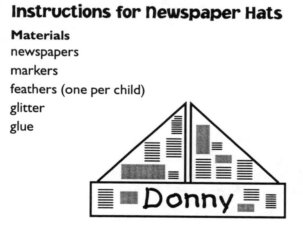

Directions

Do this as a group, one step at a time.

I. Give each child several pieces of newspaper.

2. Show them how to make it into a hat.

3. Have children use markers to print their names on their hats.

4. Let the children use glitter, markers and feather to decorate their hats. Tell them to decorate them the way they think Arthur would.

5. Put each child's hat into his/her story bag.

monkey pattern for name tag
and story bag

Someone Silly

Across:

2. Arthur sold his _____ bear to Violet.

3. Arthur's pen pal, Sandy was a _____.

4. Arthur was afraid to lose his loose _____.

5. Arthur and Violet decided to earn money by washing _____.

7. Arthur made a heart-shaped _____ in the snow.

9. The girls rescued Arthur when he got scared on a _____ out.

Down

1. _____ was Arthur's friend.

2. Arthur had a strange _____ costume.

6. Arthur was surprised to find out that Violet knew how to _____.

8. Arthur and Norman had the same _____ box.

You're Invited!

Horrible Harry's
Birthday Party!

Based on the books by Suzy Kline

Celebrate Harry's 8th Birthday: Program (60–40 minutes)

Story: *Horrible Harry in Room 2B*   Tell this story.

Project: **Make Stub People**   (Instructions on p. 79)

Game: **Pass the Presents**   (Instructions on p. 80)

Booktalks: Tell about some of the other Horrible Harry books. Choose an incident from each book. However, do not reveal the outcome of the incident. Encourage the children to read the books to find out how it gets resolved.

Story: *Horrible Harry and the Green Slime*   Tell this story.

Project: **Paint a Horrible Picture**   (Instructions on p. 80)

Snacks: Light the candles on the cake. Sing "Happy Birthday" to Harry. Blow out the candles and make a wish. Bring each child a piece of horrible cake and a cup of "bug juice."

Story Bags: Give children their story bags as they leave. Make sure they have their stub people and their "horrible prize."

I've been to Horrible Harry's birthday party at:

Planning and Promotion

Advertising Display: Have a picture of Horrible Harry holding a sign that has the program and registration information. Provide flyers with the registration and program information for people to take as reminders.

Room Decorations: Decorate the room for a birthday party. Choose a variety of silly decorations. Have funny party hats, balloons, tablecloth, plates, cups and napkins.

Nametags: Use silly (bugs, monsters) self-stick name tags.

Snacks: Have a "horrible" birthday cake. Make a white cake and add green sprinkles to the batter. Frost it with white frosting. Print "Happy Birthday, Harry" across the front of the cake. Decorate it with plastic ants. Have "bug juice" for beverages. (Use any juice you want and call it "bug juice.")

Story Bags: Give each child a brown lunch sack with a sign attached that says, **I'VE BEEN TO HORRIBLE HARRY'S BIRTHDAY PARTY AT** _____ . The children can use their bags to carry home their projects, the "horrible" prize they win playing the game, the puzzle on p. 81, and a list of the Horrible Harry materials available in your library. Party prizes can include: a silly pencil, a crazy eraser and other "horrible things."

Horrible Harry books by Suzy Kline

Books are listed in series order.

Horrible Harry in Room 2B. New York: Viking Kestral, 1988. Harry does all sorts of horrible things. He makes stub people who were planning to invade the school.

Horrible Harry and the Ant Invasion. New York: Viking Kestral, 1989. Harry has to be replaced as classroom ant monitor.

Horrible Harry and the Green Slime. New York: Viking Kestral, 1989. Harry and his classmates decorate the school with spider webs full of spiders!

Horrible Harry's Secret. New York: Viking Kestral, 1990. Harry is in love with Song Lee. It's getting way too mushy!

Horrible Harry and the Christmas Surprise. New York: Viking Kestral, 1991. Miss Mackle's chair collapses. Is Harry up to his horrible tricks again?

Horrible Harry and the Kickball Wedding. New York:: Viking Kestral, 1992. Valentine's Day is approaching and Harry cooks up all sorts of horrible things to do.

Horrible Harry and the Dungeon. New York: Viking, 1996. Harry has been sent to the Suspension Room for misbehaving.

Instructions for Stub People

Materials
crayon stubs in a variety of colors
glue
scraps of paper
scissors

Directions
Do this as a group, one step at a time

1. Give each child several crayons, glue and scraps of paper.

2. Show them how to cut out bits and pieces from the paper scraps.

3. Show them how to glue the bits of paper to the crayons to make stub people.

4. Let them create their own stub people.

5. Put each child's stub people into his/her story bag.

Instructions for Pass the Presents Game

Materials

1 very large cardboard box

small individual paper bags *(one per child)*

1 prize per child *(choose a variety of "horrible things"— rocks, sticks, dead leaves, bugs, etc.)*

tape of lively children's music and tape player

Prior to the program

1. Put a present into each bag and staple it shut.

2. Wrap the bottom and top of the large box separately. Choose "horrible" birthday wrapping paper. Stick a "horrible" bow to the lid.

3. Put the prize bags into the large box. Put the lid on it.

Directions

1. Have the children sit in a circle.

2. Play the music.

3. The children will pass the box around clockwise as the music plays.

4. When the music stops, the child holding the box will open it. The child removes a bag and puts the lid back on. That child hands the box to the next person and leaves the circle. Put each child's prize into his/her story bag.

5. Continue until all children have a "horrible prize."

Instructions for Painting a Horrible Picture

Materials

1 "daddy" shirt or smock per child

1 large sheet of white paper taped to the wall. Bottom should be at the floor.

plastic sheets and newspapers

paints in a variety of colors

5–10 squirt guns

colored markers

Prior to the program

1. Fill each squirt gun with tempera paint. Mix it so it is on the thin, watery side. Use a variety of bright colors.

2. Cover the floor with plastic and newspapers.

Directions

1. Explain that you are going to make a "horrible" picture for Horrible Harry.

2. Five children at a time may paint. The others can watch while they paint.

3. Line the children up in front of the white paper.

4. Give each child a squirt gun. Tell them to aim ONLY AT THE PAPER AND NOWHERE ELSE. Squirting at anyone or anything else will stop your turn.

5. Each child will have three squirts.

6. Say, "Ready, aim, FIRE!" On the word fire, each child may take ONE squirt.

7. Repeat this two more times.

8. Continue until each child has had a turn. You will have four groups of five children.

9. Let each child use colored marker to autograph their painting.

10. Let the mural dry for twenty-four hours.

11. Send the mural or a photograph of the mural with a letter to author, Suzy Kline (Mail to her publisher, Viking in New York). Tell her about your celebration. You can include a few photos if desired. When she responds, display her letter along with the photos of the program.

Alternatives: Have each child make their very own "horrible" painting. They can make it into a birthday card. Send all of the cards along with a letter telling about the program to the author.

Display the mural or birthday cards.

Let the children take their "horrible" pictures home.

What a mess!

Harry was supposed to make new nametags for everyone's desk. Just to be horrible, he scrambled the letters in everybody's name. Can you help fix them, so the kids know where to sit?

GOUD   Ⓞ ___ ___ ___

GONS EEL   ___ ___ ___ ___   ___ ___ ___ ___

YENDIS   Ⓞ ___ ___ ___ ___ ___

RMAY   ___ ___ ___ ___

ADI   Ⓞ ___ ___

XEDTER   ___ ___ ___ ___ ___ ___

SIMS CAKLEM   ___ ___ ___ ___   ___ ___ ___ Ⓞ ___ ___

RAYHR   ___ ___ ___ ___ ___

Print the circled letters here. _____

Unscramble them to see what they spell. ___ ___ ___ ___

You're Invited!

Mary Maroney's Birthday Party!

Based on the books by Suzy Kline

Celebrate Mary's 8th Birthday: Program (60-90 minutes)

Story: *Mary Maroney and the Snake* Tell this story.

Project: **What's in a Cone?** (Instructions on p. 84)

Story: *Mary Maroney, Mummy Girl* Tell this story.

Activity: **Mummy Wrap** (Instructions on p. 83)

Booktalks: Tell a little about the other books in the Mary Maroney series. However, do not divulge any endings. Encourage the children to read the books.

Story: *Mary Maroney and the Chocolate Surprise* Tell about the incident with the chocolate bar. However, don't divulge the outcome.

Activity: **The Contest** (Instructions on p. 83)

Snacks: At the conclusion of the contest, bring each child one small slice of pizza, a cup of water and a fizzie. Let the children drop the fizzie into the water to make their punch. When everyone is finished with their pizza, light the candles on the cake and sing "Happy Birthday" to Mary Maroney. Blow out the candles and make a wish. Bring each child a piece of cake. Refill the cups with water, and give each child another fizzie.

Story Bags: Give children a story bag as they leave. They may put their cones into the bags.

I've been to Mary Maroney's birthday party at:

Planning and Promotion

Advertising Display: Make a large poster with a picture of Mary and her friends gathered around a birthday cake. Include program and registration information on the poster. Provide flyers with the program and registration information for people to take as reminders.

Room Decorations: Decorate the room for a birthday party. Use colorful balloons, streamers, and birthday banners. Find an amusing tablecloth with matching plates, cups and napkins.

Nametags: Look for amusing (smiley face) self-stick nametags.

Snacks: Pizza, birthday cake and fizzies. Added to water fizzies make a punch like drink.

Story Bags: Have white lunch sacks. Make a sign that says, I'VE BEEN TO MARY MARONEY'S BIRTHDAY PARTY AT _____ . Children can use the bags to carry home their projects, the puzzle on p. 85 and the list of Mary Maroney materials owned by your library. Party prizes can include: fizzies, pencils, and a plastic or rubber snake.

Mary Maroney books by Suzy Kline

Books are listed in series order.

Mary Maroney and the Snake. New York: Putnam, 1992. Mary goes to a new school, where she learns to cope with her stuttering problem.

Mary Maroney Hides Out. New York: Putnam, 1993. Mary and her friends hide in the girls bathroom at school.

Mary Maroney Mummy Girl. New York: Putnam, 1994. Mary decides to dress as a mummy for Halloween.

Mary Maroney and the Chocolate Surprise. New York: Putnam, 1995. Mary cheats to win a prize at school, and ends up being the one who is surprised.

Instructions for the Contest

Materials
1 small chocolate bar per child
1 gold star per child
birthday wrapping paper
1 gift bag
1 tape of lively children's songs and tape player

Prior to the program
1. Stick a gold star to each wrapper.
2. Wrap each candy bar in birthday paper.
3. Put the candy bars into the gift bag.

Directions
1. Have the children sit in a circle. Tell the children *NOT* to open their gifts until the game is over and *EVERY-ONE* has a prize. You will give the signal when it is time to open prizes.
2. You stay on the outside of the circle.

3. Play the music. You will walk around the outside of the circle.
4. When the music stops, stop behind a child. Let that child reach into the bag and pull out a "prize."
5. That child now walks around the circle during the music, stops behind another child when the music stops and invites that child to reach into the bag.
6. Keep playing in this manner until all children have a prize.
7. Tell the children that when they open their prizes, they are to look for a gold star somewhere on their prize. If they have a gold star, it's an instant win. It means they get to have lunch with the teacher/librarian.
8. Shout, "*OPEN!*" Let the kids open their presents.
9. As soon as they discover their gold stars, bring in the pizza.
10. Continue with snacks as directed on p. 82.

Instructions for Mummy Wrap

Materials
1 extra large roll of white bathroom tissue per child *(You can ask children to bring these or ask staff members to donate a roll.)*

Prior to the program
Divide the children into groups of two. Have this planned before the program. This avoids hurt feelings among children.

Directions
Do this as a group, one step at a time.
1. Put each group of two children into a separate area.

2. Give each group one roll of tissue.
3. Child One will make Child Two into a "mummy." Show them how to do this. They will catch on quickly.
4. When all the "mummies" are wrapped, take a photo.
5. Yell, "Mummies burst out of your wrappings!" All the "mummies" can burst out.
6. Repeat the procedure. Child Two will wrap Child One.

Hint: Remind children that this is not a contest to see who gets wrapped the fastest.

Instructions for What's in a Cone?

Materials

1 piece of brown cover stock paper per child (*brown grocery bags also work*)

feathers, glitter, sequins, yarn, pom poms, fringe

movable eyes

crayons and markers

glue

stapler and staples

Prior to the program

1. Cut each piece of paper into an 8" diameter circle.

2. Cut a slit into the paper so it goes from the outside edge to the center of the paper. (Be careful not to cut paper in half.)

3. Fold circle into a cone and staple it together.

Directions

Do this as a group, one step at a time.

1. Give each child a cone. Have them use marker to print their name inside.

2. Encourage children to think of something they can make with their cone (candy holder, basket, clown hat, flower vase, unicorn, rhino horn, antler, tree, arrow, two cones will make ears, people, animals).

3. When everyone is finished, allow each child to show and tell about their cone creation.

4. Put children's projects into their story bag.

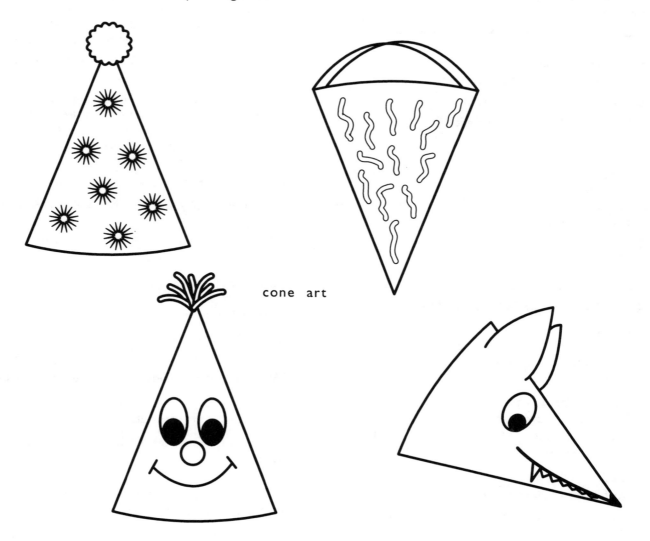

cone art

Who are they?

The names of some of the characters in the Mary Maroney stories are hidden along this path. When you find each name use a yellow marker or crayon to draw a line through it. Decorate your paper after you solve the puzzle.

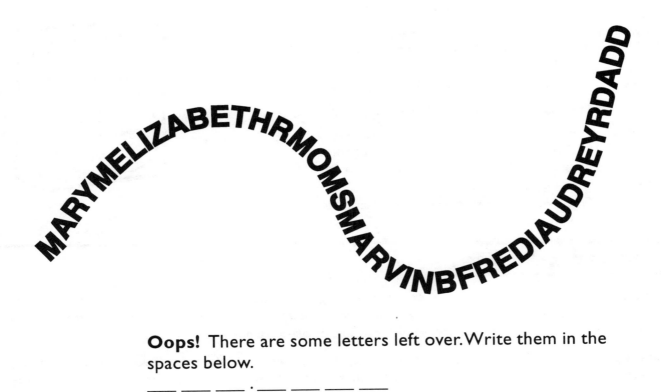

MARYMELIZABETHRMOMSMARVINBFREDIAUDREYRDADD

Oops! There are some letters left over. Write them in the spaces below.

___ ___ ___ . ___ ___ ___ ___

What is special about this?

_____

You're Invited!

Strega Nona's Birthday Party!

Based on the books by Tomie dePaola

Celebrate Strega Nona's 100th Birthday: Program (60-90 minutes)

Story: *Strega Nona, Her Story*   Read this story.

Project: **Create a Windsock**   (Instructions on p. 87)

Booktalks: Tell a little about the other Strega Nona books. Tell the story up to the climax without revealing the ending. Encourage the children to read the books.

Game: **Where Is the Magic Potion?**   (Instructions on p. 88)

Story: *Strega Nona Meets Her Match*   Read this story.

Snacks: Light the candles on the cake, and sing "Happy Birthday" to Strega Nona. Blow out the candles and make a wish. Bring each child a piece of cake and a cup of juice.

Story Bags: Give children their story bags as they leave the room.

I've been to Strega Nona's birthday party at:

Planning and Promotion

Advertising Display: Have a large, black cauldron sitting on the counter. Have fake spaghetti pouring out from the top. Have a sign with the program and registration information next to the pot. Provide cauldron shaped flyers with the program and registration information for people to take as reminders.

Room Decorations: Decorate the door to your program area with a fake door that looks like you are entering Strega Nona's cottage. Decorate the room or program area to look like the inside of her cottage. Have a false fireplace with a big magic pot sitting over the coals. Have spaghetti pouring out from the top.

Name Tags: Use the cauldron pattern on p. 88. (Five of each color: blue, green, red, yellow, orange, purple). The colors will be used to divide the children into groups for the game on p. 88. Print names on the tags.

Snacks: Have a cake with white frosting. Draw a magic pot on it. Print "Happy Birthday, Strega Nona" on it. Insert numeral candles to indicate that Strega Nona is 100 years old. Serve with juice.

Story Bags: Try to find black lunch sacks. Attach a cauldron that says, **I'VE BEEN TO STREGA NONA'S BIRTHDAY PARTY AT** _____ . The children can put the prize they win playing the game on p. 88 , their project and the puzzle on p. 89 inside their bag. Party prizes can include: anything inexpensive that is magical.

Materials and Prep

Strega Nona books by Tomie dePaola

Books are listed in series order.

Strega Nona. New York: Simon & Schuster, 1975. Big Anthony can't get the magic pot to stop making spaghetti.

Big Anthony and the Magic Ring. San Diego, CA: Harcourt Brace, 1979. Big Anthony is getting lazy. Strega Nona has to find a way to liven him up.

Strega Nona's Magic Lessons. San Diego, CA: Harcourt Brace, 1982. Big Anthony causes a big mess at the bakery.

Merry Christmas, Strega Nona. San Diego, CA: Harcourt Brace, 1986. Christmas is coming, and Strega Nona has too much to do. Can Big Anthony help her?

Strega Nona Meets Her Match. New York: Putnam, 1993. Strega Amelia has set up shop and is taking away all of Strega Nona's customers

Strega Nona, Her Story. New York: Putnam, 1996. Meet Strega Nona on the night she was born.

Instructions for Windsock

Materials
glue
staples and stapler
crayons
scissors
construction paper
paper punch

Item below are required for each child
1 12" strand of yarn
1 9" x 11" piece of cover or card stock paper
5 12" pieces of colored crepe paper strips *(blue, red, green, orange, purple)*

Directions
Do this as a group, one step at a time.

1. Give each child a piece of yellow card or cover stock paper and some crayons.

2. Show them how to place the paper horizontally on the table.

3. Tell them to draw a picture of their favorite happening in a Strega Nona story.

4. Help them roll the paper so they make a tube. Staple at the top and bottom.

5. Give each child a piece of white construction paper. Tell them to draw a picture of one important item from each story (ring, pot)

6. Have them cut out the pictures.

7. Give each child five colored strips of crepe paper.

8. Tell them to glue one picture to the end of each piece of crepe paper.

9. Tell them to glue the other end of the crepe paper strips around the bottom of the windsock.

10. Use the paper punch to punch two holes in the top of the windsock.

11. Help the children string the yarn through the holes and tie it at the top, so they can hang their windsocks.

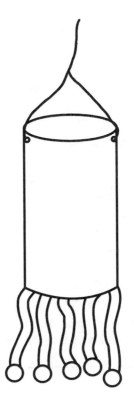

windsock

Instructions for Where is the Magic Potion?

Materials

1 black cauldron

1 small bottle of hand lotion per child *(Ask a local hotel for a donation or purchase the grocery store samples.)*

5 stars *(blue, red, green, yellow, orange, purple)*

5 circles *(blue, red, green, yellow, orange, purple)*

5 diamonds *(blue, red, green, yellow, orange, purple)*

5 rectangles *(blue, red, green, yellow, orange, purple)*

5 ovals *(blue, red, green, yellow, orange, purple)*

5 squares *(blue, red, green, yellow, orange, purple)*

Prior to the program

1. Put the bottles of magic potion into the cauldron and hide it well.

2. Make a treasure hunt for the children. The name tags will divide them into teams of five players each. Each team will follow the color trail that matches their name tag. There is a sample treasure hunt for the blue team below.

3. Be sure to have a different order for each trail.

4. On each shape you will draw another shape. That will tell the team what shape to look for next.

5. Hide the shapes well.

Directions

1. Tell each group of children to find their partners. "Partners will have the same color nametag as you do." Have each group gather in a separate area.

2. Tell them to follow the trail. "The trail is the same color as your nametag. It is important to look carefully at each shape. It will tell you which shape to look for next. Soon you will be at your last clue location. You will find a special prize hidden there. Quietly, take ONE and return to the program area."

3. Assign one person on each team to collect each shape as they find it.

   Hint: Have a staff member or helper stay with each group.

Sample Hunt for the Blue Team

Clue 1: Look for a blue star.
   [Hide it the fairy tale section.]

Clue 2: A square is drawn on the blue star.
   [Hide the blue square in the audiovisual section.]

Clue 3: A diamond is drawn on the blue square.
   [Hide the blue diamond in the sports (796) area of the non-fiction books.]

Clue 4: A rectangle is drawn on the blue diamond.
   [Hide the blue rectangle in the magazine section.]

Clue 5: An oval is drawn on the blue rectangle.
   [Hide the blue oval by the picture books— authors names beginning with B.]

Clue 6: A circle is drawn on the blue oval.
   [Hide the blue circle in the 793 area. The magic pot will be here. This is where they will find their magic potion.]

Clue 7: When You Find Your Bottle of Magic Potion, Return to the Program Area.

⤴Arrange a hunt for each group. Have each group go in a different order. For example, use different sections of each area they visit. The final clue will bring everyone to the same place. Start each group one minute later than the previous group. That will ease some of the congestion.

Patterns

cauldron for name tag and story bag

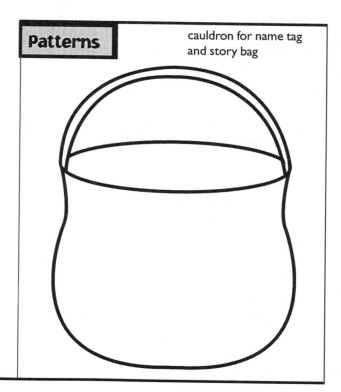

Help!

Oh, no! The magic pot has bubbled over. There is spaghetti all over the place. Try to eat your way out!

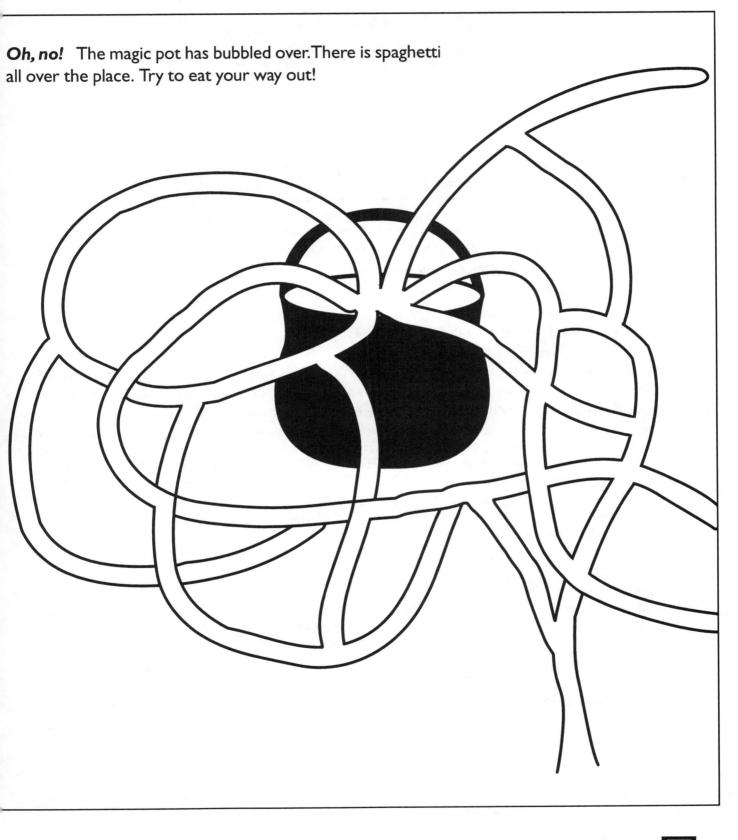

You're Invited!

Nate the Great's Birthday Party!

Based on the books by
Marjorie Weinman Sharmat

Celebrate Nate's 8th Birthday: Program (60-90 minutes)

Story: *Nate the Great* Introduce Nate the Great and have him help tell this story. Ask Nate if he has solved other mysteries. He can tell you that there was a time when color played an important part in a story. If you are doing the program without Nate, tell the children that Nate visited one day and told you about this fascinating case.

Activity: **The Mystery of the Mixed Colors** (Instructions on p. 93)

Story: *Nate the Great and the Stolen Base* Read this story.

Game: **What's Next?** (Instructions on p. 93)

Story: *Nate the Great and the Pillowcase* Read this story.

Project: **Make a Detective Bag** (Instructions on p. 91)

Booktalks: Select several books from the other Nate the Great books. Tell a little about each mystery, but do not reveal the outcome. Encourage children to check out the book and read it to discover how the case is solved.

Activity: **Solve the Mystery of the Missing Party Prizes** (Instructions on p. 92)

Snacks: There is one more mystery to be solved. The cake was supposed to have multi-colored sprinkles on top of the frosting. And, there was supposed to be a cherry on top of each scoop of ice cream. When the cook was preparing the items, he/she found these items missing. Light the candles, and sing "Happy Birthday' to Nate. Blow out the candles and make a wish. Of course, the children will discover the missing items when they eat their snacks.

Detective Bags: Add the puzzle (p. 95) and your list of Nate the Great materials to the bags. When you add the puzzle, it should be folded in half and stapled shut. Tell the children you are giving them another mystery to solve at home.

Planning and Promotion

Advertising Display: Have a cutout of Nate the Great with a magnifying glass and stand him beside a poster with the program information on it. Have him using the magnifying glass to magnify a portion of the program information. Include flyers with registration information for people to take as reminders.

Room Decorations: Decorate the room with banners, balloons and streamers. Try to find a tablecloth, plates, napkins and cups with a mystery or detective theme. Include items from the Nate the Great stories.

Guest Character: Get a talented junior high or high school student to dress as Nate and help with the program.

Name Tags: Use the magnifying glass pattern on p. 91 On the back of each tag, tape a small piece of paper with one letter from the title, "Nate the Great and the Pillowcase" (See What's Next, p. 93). Use both sets of quotation marks. That allows for 30 characters. If you have fewer than 30 children, fill in some of the letters of the puzzle in advance.

Snacks: Have birthday cake and vanilla ice cream. Make a white cake and add multi-colored sprinkles to the batter. Frost the cake with white frosting. Draw a magnifying glass on the cake, and insert eight candles. Put a cherry under each scoop of ice cream. These two steps are important, so be sure to include them. Serve juice for beverages.

Planning and Promotion

Camera & Film: Have an instant camera ready and take a detective photo of each child as he/she arrives.

Case Books: Give each child a case book (see p. 94) with his/her photo inside *(This is the photo you take when they arrive).* Have a black stamp pad available. Let each child put their thumb print in the space provided. Have children fill in the information called for in the book. Provide a measuring tape and scale so that you can weigh and measure each "detective." Set the books aside and give them to the children when it is time for the Mystery hunt (p. 92-93).

Detective Bags: Have children decorate their detective bags (p.91). The children will search for their party prizes: a pencil with red lead, a small magnifying glass, and a small notebook. The clues to finding these items are on p. 92. Give them the puzzle on p. 95 and a list of Nate the Great materials available in your library.

Materials

Nate the Great books by Marjorie Weinman Sharmat

Nate the Great. New York: Coward, McCann & Geoghegan, 1972. Nate is asked to find a missing picture.

Nate the Great Goes Undercover. New York: Coward, McCann & Geoghegan, 1974. There's a garbage snatcher in town. It might Nate take all night to catch the culprit.

Nate the Great and the Lost List. New York: Coward, McCann & Geoghegan, 1975. They need to find the missing grocery list before lunch, or there won't be any lunch.

Nate the Great and the Phony Clue. New York: Coward, McCann & Geoghegan, 1977. Nate has only part of the clue. If he can find the rest of it, he might be able to solve the case.

Nate the Great and the Sticky Case. New York: Coward, McCann & Geoghegan, 1978. Claude's stegosaurus stamp is missing. Can Nate find it?

Nate the Great and the Missing Key. New York: Coward, McCann & Geoghegan, 1981. Annie has lost her house key and can't get into her house. How can she set up for the party?

Nate the Great and the Snowy Trail. New York: Coward, McCann & Geoghegan, 1982. Rosamond lost Nate's birthday present. It looks like Nate is going to have to find his own gift.

Nate the Great and the Fishy Prize. New York: Coward-McCann, 1985. Nate is planning to enter Sludge in a dog contest, but the winning prize has been stolen.

Nate the Great Stalks Superweed. New York: Coward-McCann, 1986. Olivia's weed has vanished. Nate sets out to find out where it has gone.

Nate the Great and the Boring Beach Bag. New York: Coward-McCann, 1987. Oliver's beach bag has vanished. Who could have take it?

Nate the Great Goes Down in the Dumps. New York: Coward-McCann, 1987. Rosamond's money box is missing. Can Nate discover what's happened?

Nate the Great and the Halloween Hunt. New York: Coward-McCann, 1989. Nate and Sludge are locked up in a haunted house when they try to solve a Halloween mystery.

Nate the Great and the Musical Note. New York: Coward-McCann, 1990. There's a note with a secret meaning. It has something to do with a music lesson.

Nate the Great and the Stolen Base. New York: Coward-McCann, 1992. Second base has been stolen. Can Nate find the thief?

Nate the Great and the Missing Pillowcase. New York: Delacorte Press, 1993. Big Heg's pillowcase has disappeared. Can Nate discover what has happened to it?

Nate the Great and the Mushy Valentine. New York: Delacorte Press, 1994. There's a missing Valentine and a mystery Valentine that came from nowhere. What's going on?

Instructions for Detective Bag

Materials
1 brown lunch sack per child
crayons and markers
pre-made sign that says: **I'VE BEEN TO NATE the GREAT'S BIRTHDAY PARTY AT _____.**

Prior to the program
Glue the sign on one side of each bag.

Directions
1. Give each child a bag.
2. Tell them this is their Detective Bag. Let them use crayons and markers to decorate it. Make sure they print their name on it.

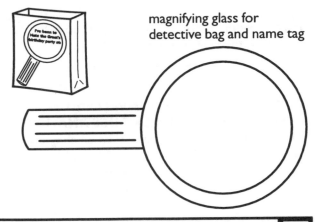

magnifying glass for detective bag and name tag

Instructions for the Mystery of the Missing Party Prizes

Materials

1 red pencil per child

1 small, plastic magnifying glass per child

1 small notebook per child

1 helper/team leader per group (*room parents, older children, volunteers, staff members, etc.*)

clue envelopes

Prior to the program

1. Divide the children into small groups of three to five children each. Have teams made up before children arrive. When doing this with one age group, arrange the children so that you have different abilities within each group. When doing this with a mixed age group, put kindergartners, 1st graders and 2nd graders in each group.

2. Avoid allowing children to choose their own groups. Follow the rule, "The team you are assigned to is the team you are on."

3. Meet with your Team Leaders prior to the program to explain how the Mystery Hunt works. If possible, do a run through, so everyone knows where to go.

4. Prepare the clue envelopes. Give these to the Team Leaders at the beginning of the hunt.

5. Team Leaders will give out each envelope at the proper time.

6. So you do not have all of the teams going in the same direction at the same time, follow this order of clues.

Teams 1 and 4	Envelopes 1, 2, 3
Teams 2 and 5	Envelopes 2, 3, 1
Teams 3 and 6	Envelopes 3, 1, 2

Have teams 4, 5 & 6 start 3 minutes after teams 1, 2 & 3.

Paper clip each group of envelopes together in the proper order. Tell the team leaders not to change the order of them.

Directions

1. Remind children and Team Leaders that this is not a race to see who gets finished first. Everyone will have a chance to solve the mystery and find their party prizes.

   You can remind children of this by saying, "Stop! This is not a race. Everyone will get their prizes."

2. Give the clue envelopes to the Team Leaders of Teams 1, 2 and 3. Tell the children to stay with their Team Leader.

3. Send Teams 1, 2 and 3 on their way. Tell them to open the top envelope to reveal the first clue. They will find something at that location. Follow the directions at each location.

4. Wait three minutes. Send Teams 4, 5 and 6 out with the same instructions.

5. When all teams have returned, continue with the program.

Clue Envelopes

Envelope 1: This message will be printed on the front of the envelope.

> ### DO NOT OPEN THIS ENVELOPE UNTIL YOU REACH YOUR DESTINATION
> Go to the place where you check out library materials. What is this counter called? Take this envelope to the people there. Ask one of them to help you decipher the clue inside this envelope.

> ### DO NOT OPEN THIS ENVELOPE UNTIL YOU REACH YOUR NEXT DESTINATION
> The people here greet people when they come into the building. Go to that desk. They will help you decipher the clue inside the envelope.

Envelope 3: This message will be printed on the front of the envelope.

> ### DO NOT OPEN THIS ENVELOPE UNTIL YOU REACH YOUR DESTINATION
> The people at this desk help children solve mysteries (helping with assignments, finding good books). What is this desk called? Go to that desk and ask the people there to help you solve this mystery.

Envelope 2: This message will be printed on the front of the envelope.

Solutions to the Nate the Great Mystery Hunt

Envelope 1: Takes children to the circulation/check out desk. Inside the envelope are individual letter squares that spell out the word **PENCIL**. The people at the desk will give each child a red-leaded pencil.

Envelope 2: Inside this envelope is a backwards message. Hold it up to a mirror to decipher it. The words **magnifying glass** will be written backwards in cursive. The person at this desk gives each child a magnifying glass.

Envelope 3: Inside this envelope is a rebus. (Draw this on a piece of paper.) The people at the children's reference desk will give each child a small notebook.

Envelope 4: After all three envelopes are opened and solved, the Team Leader can present the children with a fourth envelope. Inside the envelope is this message. The children will have to unscramble the words to decipher the message. Do this together as a group.

> Now it is EMIT_____ to do GNIHTEMOS _____ new.
> Sit in a ELCRIC _____ on the floor and answer these questions.
> What do you like to eat at a birthday YTRAP _____? If you like birthday EKAC _____ raise your right hand. If you like ECI ____ MAERC _____ raise you left hand. Now be as quiet as possible and return to your seats.

Hints: Have children put prizes into their detective bags as they receive them. Lost prizes are lost prizes.

If necessary, tell children that the scrambled messages are all just spelled backwards. To unscramble, start at the end.

Case Book patterns are found on p. 94. Add blank pages for the children to solve their own mysteries. Staple case books together for children.

Instructions for the Mystery of the Mixed Colors

Materials
blue tempera paint
red tempera paint
2 paint brushes
paper
easel or use flannelboard covered with paper

Directions
1. Attach a piece of paper to the easel or board.
2. Ask two children to come up and help you.
3. Let one child put a circle of blue paint in the middle of the paper.
4. Let the second child put a circle of red paint on top of the blue paint and mix.
5. What happens? The paint becomes purple.
6. Take the paint brush and transform the circle into a purple octopus.

   This leads to the next story, *Nate the Great and the Stolen Base.*

Instructions for What's Next? Game

Materials
1 shoe box covered with contact paper. Make a slit in the lid.

1 small piece of gray paper, cut to fit inside the lid. *Tape it inside the lid. You want it to look like part of the lid, but be just loose enough for the pieces to rattle around inside it when you shake the box. Make sure the pieces cannot fall out when you shake the box. The pieces will be inside the secret compartment and will not go down inside the box.*

letter squares attached to the back of each nametag. *(See Name Tags on p. 90)*

35 small pieces of gray paper. *Print one letter or set of quotation marks on each piece of paper. There will be five pieces left over. These are the spaces between words. Join these together so they show the title of the story. Tape them together across the back. Lay this across the bottom of the box. If you have fewer than 30 children, have some letters inside the box top already.*

Directions
1. Tell the children to look on the backs of their name tags.
2. When they spot the letters, ask them to carefully remove them and put them into your "Mystery Box."
3. Shake the box. Open the lid and pull out the gray piece of paper with the title of the next story on it.
4. Put the box away out of reach of the children, so they do not discover your secret.

Detective

_____'s

(First Name) (Last Name)

Case **Book**

Case Book cover

Detectives Name:

_____
(First)   (Last)

Birthdate: _____ _____ _____
               (Month) (Day)   (Year)

Age: _____ years old

Eye Color: _____

Hair Color: _____

Weight: _____ pounds

Height: _____ feet _____ inches

photo

thumb print

Detective Identification page

Dear Detectives:

The prizes for Nate the Great's birthday party were lost, but you helped find them. Print the details of the case neatly in the spaces below.

I solved the case of "The Missing Party Prizes."
I found the _____ at
the _____. The
_____
was at the _____. I went to
the _____ where I
found the _____.
I also found the missing sprinkles and cherries.
The sprinkles were found
_____
and the cherries were found
_____.

Hints:

1. Enlarge these pages.

2. Include several blank pages for children to add their own mysteries.

Mystery Hunt recording page

What is nate searching for?

What Is Nate Searching For?
Several items are still missing. Can you help Nate find them. Use your red pencil to color in the spaces marked with an N. Print the names of the items you found in the spaces. ___◯___ , ___◯◯ , ◯___ ___◯ , ◯___◯___ ,
___◯___◯___◯___ ___ ___ ___ , ___ ___ ___◯ ,
___◯◯___ ___ ___ ___ ___◯___ ___

Print the circled letters here. _____

Unscramble them:

___ ___ ___ ___   ___ ___ ___   ___ ___ ___ ___ ___ is quite clever!

You're Invited!

Frances Badger's Birthday Party!

Based on the books by Russell Hoban

Celebrate Frances' 6th Birthday: Program (60-90 minutes)

Story: *Best Friends for Frances* Make this into a flannelboard story.

Project: **Make Birthday Cards for Frances** (Instructions on p. 97)

Story: *Bread and Jam for Frances* Read this story.

Poem: "Stone Kicking Song" From: *Egg Thoughts and Other Frances Songs.*

Game: **Stone Kicking Game** (Instructions on p. 97)

Story: *A Bargain for Frances* Read this story.

Project: **Make a Frances Badger Mask** (Instructions on p. 98-99)

Booktalks: Choose some of the other Frances Badger books. Present short book talks on each of them. However, do not reveal the endings. Encourage the children to read the books to find out how they end.

Snacks: Light the candles on the cake. Sing "Happy Birthday" to Frances and blow out the candles. Bring each child a piece of cake and a cup of lemonade.

Story Bags: Give each child a story bag. Make sure their masks are inside them.

Planning and Promotion

Advertising Display: Have a cutout of Frances holding a sign with the program and registration information. Provide flyers for people to take as reminders.

Room Decorations: Decorate the room with animal-themed birthday party decorations. Have balloons, streamers and Happy Birthday banners.

Name Tags: Use the badger-shaped nametag on p. 98.

Snacks: Have a birthday cake with six candles. Print Happy Birthday, Frances! across the top. Decorate it with miniature candy bars. Have one candy bar per child attending the party. Serve lemonade for the beverage.

Story Bags: Have a white lunch sack with a badger cutout attached. (p. 98). Print **I'VE BEEN TO FRANCES BADGER'S BIRTHDAY PARTY AT** _____ .The children can use the bag to carry home their masks and the puzzle on p. 100. Party prizes can include small package of jam, colored stones, mini candy bar from the cake etc.

Materials and Prep

Frances books by Russell Hoban

Books are listed in series order.

Bedtime for Frances. New York: Harper & Row, 1960. Frances does everything she can think of to keep from going to bed.

Egg Thoughts and Other Frances Songs. New York: Harper & Row, 1964. This is a book of the songs Frances likes to sing.

A Baby Sister for Frances. New York: Harper & Row, 1964. Frances is jealous of her baby sister, Gloria.

Bread and Jam for Frances. New York: Harper & Row, 1964/1992. All Frances likes to eat is bread and jam. But one day she gets sick of it.

A Birthday for Frances. New York: Harper & Row, 1968. Frances doesn't want to celebrate her sister's birthday.

Best Friends for Frances. New York: Harper & Row, 1969/1994, Frances learns some important things about friendship.

A Bargain for Frances. New York: Harper & Row, 1970. Frances and her friend, Thelma make a bargain that doesn't work out.

Instructions for Making Birthday Cards for Frances

Materials
1 copy of the nametag pattern per child (p. 98)
crayons
staples and stapler

Directions
Do this as a group, one step at a time.

1. Give each child the nametag pattern.
2. Let them color the front.
3. Have them write a birthday message on the back and sign their name.

4. Send the cards to author Russell Hoban. Include a note from you telling about your program. If he replies, display his letter along with photos from your program.

Alternative: Display the cards for others to enjoy.

Hints: Help children as needed with writing a message and signing their names.

Instructions for Stone Kicking Game

Materials
several stones
adhesive tape
animal bookmarks (badgers if possible)

Prior to the Program
1. Have one tape line for children to stand behind.
2. Have another tape line across the room.

Directions
1. One at a time, let each child stand behind the line and kick a stone.
2. When a child gets the stone across the line, they win an animal bookmark. (Some children may need more than one turn. Let them know this is okay.)

Hints: Adjust the distance as needed depending upon the size and age of each child.

Instructions for Making a Badger Mask

Materials

1 badger head per child (p.99) *This should be run on beige cover or card stock paper.*

1 paint stick per child

black, brown, gray and white crayons

glue

scissors

pencils

Prior to the program

Cut out masks.

Directions

Do this as a group, one step at a time.

1. Give each child a mask.

2. Hold the mask up to each child's face. Use pencil to mark the eye holes. Help children to cut out their eyes holes.

3. Let the children use the black crayon to draw a nose on the badger.

4. Give the children the brown, gray and white crayons and let them color the rest of the badger's face.

5. Glue each child's badger to their paint stick.

6. Children can hold the mask up to their faces and pretend to be badgers.

Patterns

badger pattern for name tag,
story bag and birthday card

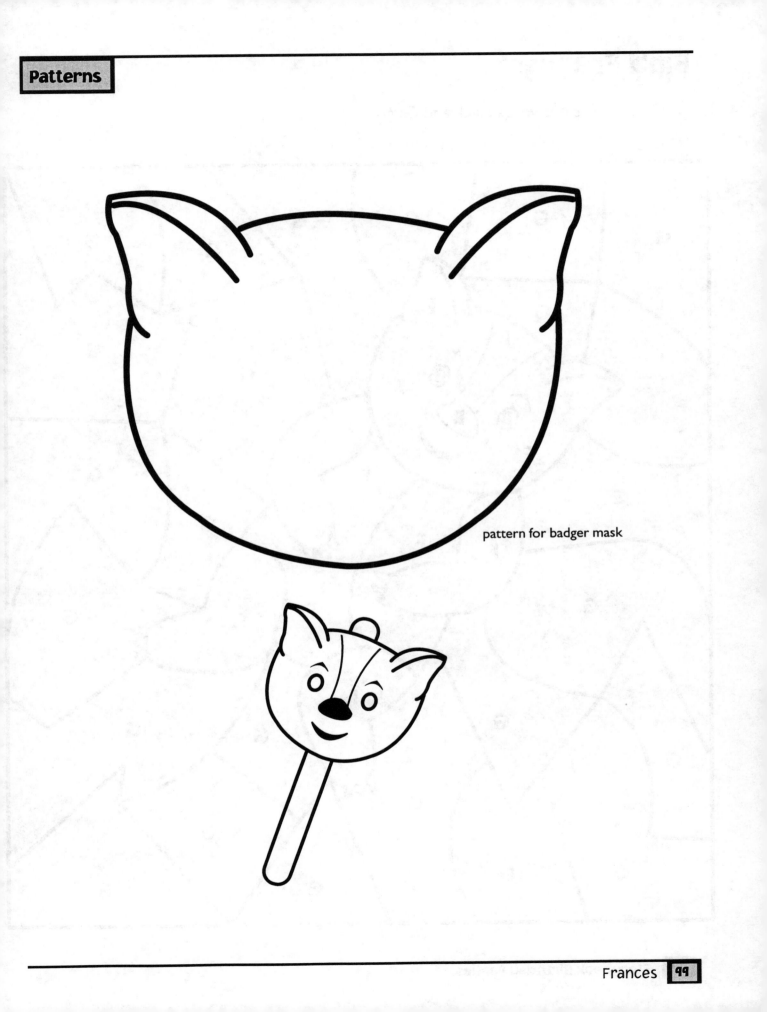

pattern for badger mask

Find Frances

Color the Fs brown, Bs black and Gs green.

Storybook Birthday Parties

You're Invited!

Amanda Pig's
Birthday Party!

Based on the books by Jean Van Leeuwen

Celebrate Amanda's 5th Birthday: Program (60-90 minutes)

Story: *Tales of Amanda Pig* Read this story.

Project: **Making Kites** (Instructions on p. 103)

Booktalks: Choose one incident from each of the Amanda Pig books you don't read in the program. Tell the incident up to the climax, but don't reveal the ending. Encourage children to read the books to find out how the incidents are resolved.

Game: **Pigs in the Puddle** (Instructions on p. 102)

Story: *Amanda Pig, Schoolgirl* Read this story.

Snacks: Light the candles on the cake, and sing "Happy Birthday" to Amanda Pig. Blow out the candles and make a wish.

Story Bags: Give children their story bags as they leave the room. Make sure they have their kites.

Planning and Promotion

Advertising Display: Have a poster with Amanda Pig playing ball. Oliver can be flying a kite in the sky. Print the program and registration information on the ball and kite. Have kite-shaped flyers with the program and registration information for people to take as reminders.

Room Decorations: Decorate the room to look like Amanda and Oliver's play room. Have toys, kites etc. Try to find a tablecloth, napkins, cups and plates with a pig theme.

Nametags: Use the kite pattern on p. 103.

Snacks: Have a birthday cake with Amanda and Oliver on it. Have them flying kites. Write **HAPPY BIRTHDAY, AMANDA PIG** on the cake. Have juice for the beverage. Insert five candles into the cake.

Story Bags: Have brown lunch sacks. Attach a kite that says, **I'VE BEEN TO AMANDA PIG'S BIRTHDAY PARTY AT** _____ . The children can use these to carry home the projects they make on p. 103, the prize they win playing the game on p. 102, the puzzle on p. 104 and the bookmark listing the Amanda Pig materials owned by your library. Party prizes can include anything related to pigs or items that remind you of the stories.

Amanda Pig books by Jean Van Leeuwen

Books are listed in series order.

Amanda Pig and Her Big Brother Oliver. New York: Puffin, 1982. Amanda and her brother have fun playing together.

Tales of Amanda Pig. New York: Dial Books for Young Readers, 1983. Amanda and Oliver spend a busy autumn day helping their parents.

More Tales of Amanda Pig. New York: Dial Books for Young Readers, 1985. Amanda and her brother Oliver have some silly adventures as they play together.

Oliver, Amanda and Grandmother Pig. New York: Dial Books for Young Readers, 1987. Grandmother comes to visit Amanda and Oliver.

Amanda Pig On Her Own. New York: Dial Books for Young Readers, 1991. When Oliver goes to school, Amanda has to learn to play alone.

Oliver and Amanda and the Big Snow. New York: Dial Books for Young Readers, 1995. Amanda and Oliver have fun playing in the snow.

Amanda Pig, Schoolgirl. New York: Dial Books for Young Readers, 1997. At last, Amanda is big enough to go to school. What fun!

The Oliver Pig books also feature Amanda.

Instructions for Pigs in the Puddle

Materials

audiocassette tape of silly children's songs and audio-cassette player

masking tape

laminating film and machine or clear contact paper

wrapping paper and ribbons

individually wrapped candies

One of each item below per child

1 puddle per child cut from blue construction paper

1 bathroom tissue roll per child

1 silly prize per child (they need to fit inside bathroom tissue rolls)

Prior to the program

1. Laminate the puddles. (This allows you to reuse them.)

2. Put a piece of rolled masking tape on the back of each puddle.

3. Put one prize inside each tissue roll. Include several pieces of individually wrapped candies.

4. Wrap the rolls and tie the ends with ribbons.

Directions

1. Place the puddles on the floor.

2. Tell each child to find a puddle to stand on.

3. Play the music. Tell the children to walk around the room. When the music stops they are to find a puddle to stand on.

4. Stop the music. Everyone should be on a puddle.

5. Tell the children the sun came up and dried up one of the puddles. Remove a puddle.

6. Play the music. Let the children walk around the room. Stop the music. Tell the children to find a puddle. One child will be without a puddle. That child can reach into the sack and pull out a prize to put inside their story bag.

7. Continue playing until all of the puddles are dried up and everyone has a prize.

8. Tell the children to wait until they get home to open their party prizes.

Instructions for Making Kites

Materials
1 large, brown grocery bag per child
1 24" crepe paper streamer per child
scraps of colorful paper
pieces of material
yarn
glitter
glue
paper punch

Prior to the program
Cut each paper bag so it will lay flat. Then cut each into a kite shape.

Directions
1. Give each child a kite.
2. Tell the children to use the materials to decorate both sides of their kite.
3. Show them how to attach the tail to the bottom.
4. Punch a hole in the top and attach a piece of yarn.
5. Have the children print their names on their kites. They can take them home.

kite pattern for the name tag, kite and story bag

Lost Toys

Amanda has lost some of her toys. Can you find her ball,
her kite, her sled, her bunny, and her wagon? When you find
them, color them.

Parties for 3rd – 5th Grades

The parties in this section are designed for children in grades 3 – 5. Children attend without parents. You can have between twenty and thirty children at each program. If you are hosting this party in a public library or bookstore, it is advisable to request that parents remain in the building during the program. That allows you to find a child's parents in case of an emergency.

The parties include stories, activities, games and projects relating to the character's birthday. Of course, birthday refreshments will be served. Let parents know that food will be served. Some children are on special diets. Be willing to make substitutions for these children, or have a child's parent supply a suitable snack.

With the varied schedules people have today, it is recommended that you offer a variety of times for the parties. After school, evenings, weekends and school holidays allow you to meet the needs of many people. Try to offer several sessions of each party if you serve a large population.

Try to follow the order and format of each party. Each program has been carefully designed to enhance the children's enjoyment of each story.

Rather than focusing on the "popular today, gone tomorrow" characters, these parties are for characters who have lasting appeal. These parties serve as a good introduction to several new series for children.

Celebrate and have fun!

The objectives for these parties include:

- Introduce the children to new book characters

- Increase listening and reading skills

- Encourage creativity through art and writing activities

- Develop library skills (treasure hunts)

- Encourage an enjoyment of books and reading

You're Invited!

Gwen's Birthday Party!

Based on the books by Elizabeth Levy

Celebrate Gwen's 10th Birthday: Program (90 minutes–2 hours)

Story: *Something Queer Is Going On* Jill and Gwen can tell this story to the children.

Activity: **Find Fletcher** (Instructions on p. 107)

Story: *Something Queer at the Library* Read this story.

Project: **Make Birthday Banners** (Instructions on p. 108)

Booktalks: Encourage the children to read other books in this series by telling a bit about each story. Tell just enough to entice the children to read them on their own.

Story: *Something Queer at the Birthday Party* Jill and Gwen can tell this story. When they're finished, ask them get the story bags and snacks. They'll return and tell you that the presents and food are missing! The children will need to search for them.

> 1 Pencil
> 1 Notebook
> 1 Package of Lemonade
> 1 Puzzle

Activity: **Birthday Present Hunt** (Instructions on p. 108)

Snacks: While the children are out of the room, have someone fill the glasses with lemonade. Put a gummy fish and a couple of pieces of ice in each glass, and then keep these out of sight till later. When the children return with their story bags full of prizes, have them sit down. Gwen and Jill will return in a few minutes with the cake and ice cream. Have them give clues about where they found these. See if the children can guess. Light the candles and sing "Happy Birthday" to Gwen. She can blow out the candles. Give each child a piece of cake with ice cream and a glass of lemonade. Watch their reactions when they find fish swimming in their lemonade.

Story Bags: Make sure the children have their story bags filled with the treasures they found. Have them take their banners and bookmarks listing the "Something Queer" materials too.

Planning and Promotion

Advertising Display: Use a large stuffed dog. Have it lying next to a poster that has the program and registration information on it. Provide individual flyers for people to take as reminders.

Room Decorations: Decorate using streamers, banners, balloons, etc. If possible, have a stuffed dog to portray Fletcher. Try to find a tablecloth, plates and napkins on a mystery theme. Use clear, plastic glasses for the lemonade.

Guest Characters: Have two staff members dress up and portray Gwen and Jill. They can lead the children through some of the activities.

Name Tags: Use any self-stick nametags. Try to find a birthday or mystery theme.

Planning and Promotion

Snacks: Have birthday cake and ice cream. Print **HAPPY BIRTHDAY, GWEN** on the cake. Insert ten candles. For the beverage, serve lemonade with gummy fish swimming in it. Serve the lemonade in clear, plastic glasses.

Story Bags: Supply one lunch bag per child. Attach a typed list of the things they will have to locate on the "Birthday Present Hunt." (p. 108) These include: pencil, little notebook, package of lemonade mix, and the puzzle on p. 109. Also give each child a bookmark listing the "Something Queer" materials available in your library. On the other side of the bag, write the words, **I'VE BEEN TO GWEN'S BIRTHDAY PARTY AT** _____ .

> I've been to
> Gwen's
> birthday party at:

Materials and Prep

Gwen books by Elizabeth Levy

Books are listed in series order.

Something Queer Is Going On. New York: Dell, 1982, 1973. Jill's dog Fletcher is missing. What's happened to him?

Something Queer at the Ball Park. New York: Dell, 1994, 1975. Jill's lucky baseball bat is missing. Gwen sets out to see if she can find it.

Something Queer at the Library. New York: Dell 1988, 1977. Jill and Gwen discover that someone has been cutting dog pictures out of library books. They have to find the culprit, so the librarian won't accuse them of this horrible act of vandalism.

Something Queer on Vacation. New York: Dell, 1982, 1980. Jill and Gwen are determined to win the sand castle building contest, but someone keeps destroying their castles.

Something Queer at the Haunted School. New York: Dell, 1983, 1982. Gwen and Jill are working on their Halloween costumes when they hear a horrible scream. What has happened?

Something Queer at the Lemonade Stand. New York; Delacorte, 1982. Jill and Gwen open a lemonade stand, but something strange has happened to the lemonade.

Something Queer in Rock 'n Roll. New York: Delacorte, 1987. Gwen and Jill need Fletcher to howl about the pizza, but Fletcher seems to have lost all interest in pizza. What's wrong with that dog?

Something Queer at the Birthday Party. New York: Delacorte Press, 1990. Jill wants to surprise Gwen on her birthday, but it's Jill who gets surprised.

Something Queer in Outer Space. New York: Hyperion Books for Children, 1993. Fletcher was going into outer space. It looked as though someone was trying to hurt him

Something Queer in the Cafeteria. New York: Hyperion Books for Children, 1994. All sorts of things are going wrong in the new school cafeteria. Gwen and Jill are being blamed for everything, but they haven't done anything wrong.

Something Queer at the Scary Movie. New York: Hyperion Books for Children, 1995. Gwen and Jill are making a scary movie during summer vacation. It turns out to be scarier than they had planned.

Instructions for Find Fletcher

Materials
1 large stuffed dog to portray Fletcher

Prior to the program
Hide Fletcher in a hard to discover place.

Directions
1. Divide the children into two groups. Have groups

made up prior to the program. Avoid letting the children choose their own groups.

2. Have one group go with Gwen, the other go with Jill.

3. See which group can find Fletcher and bring him back.

Instructions for Birthday Banners

Materials

1 12" x 18" piece of pastel-colored, heavy duty construction paper per child *(Fold down the top inch of paper.)*

paper cutouts in a variety of colorful & interesting shapes

glitter

glue

crayons and pencils

staples and stapler or tape.

Directions

Do this as a group, one step at a time.

1. Give each child a large piece of paper. Have children print their names on the paper.

2. Let the children use the crayons, paper shapes and glitter to create a birthday banner for Gwen.

3. Give each child a hanger. Have them "hang" the banners on the hanger. The fold will help them. Staple or tape the fold down in back, so the banner stays put.

4. Let the banners dry during the program.

5. Children can take these home at the end of the program.

Alternatives: Hang the banners for others to enjoy. After a couple of weeks, take them down, and let the children take them home.

Instructions for the Birthday Present Hunt

Materials

1 paper bag per child *See story bags on p. 107. Have a list of the missing items attached to the bag.*

30 of each item: pencil, eraser, little notebook, packet of lemonade mix, star stickers, and a rolled piece of paper with the puzzle on it. (p. 109)

birthday stickers

Prior to the program

1. Hide the items throughout the area where children will search. Hide them well and keep them out of view.

2. Place a small birthday sticker at each location to alert children that this is one of the locations.

Directions

1. Give each child a paper bag.

2. Tell the children they must locate the missing items listed on the back. Go over this list together, so everyone understands what to look for,

3. Caution the children to keep prize locations secret once they find an item.

4. Tell the children that they may take only one of each item.

5. Tell the children to return to the party area as soon as they have found all of the items.

Hints:

1. Vary the order in which you list the items on the bags. This keeps the kids scattered about.

2. Hide all of the pencils in the same place, all of the notebooks in the same place, etc.

3. Try to have staff members, volunteers or parent helpers "near" each location to make sure kids take only one of each prize. They can also provide reading assistance as needed.

Something queer has happened!

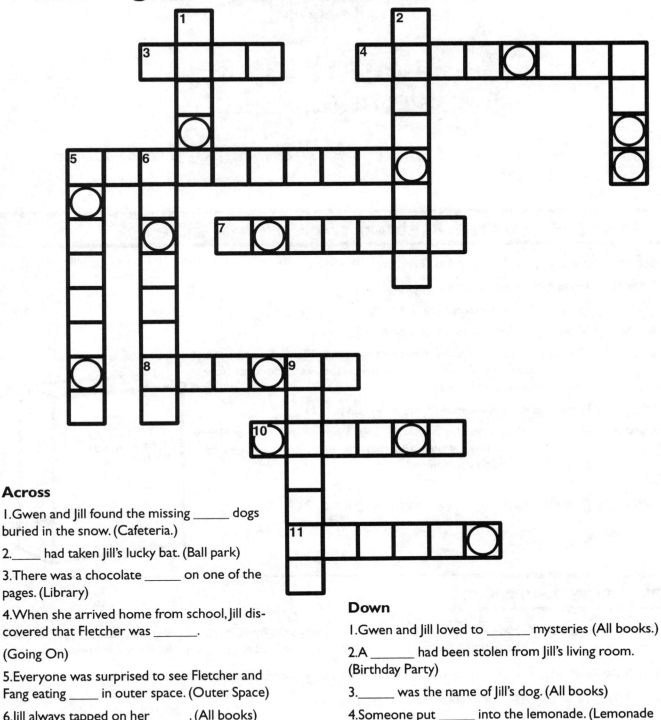

Across

1. Gwen and Jill found the missing _____ dogs buried in the snow. (Cafeteria.)

2. _____ had taken Jill's lucky bat. (Ball park)

3. There was a chocolate _____ on one of the pages. (Library)

4. When she arrived home from school, Jill discovered that Fletcher was _____.
(Going On)

5. Everyone was surprised to see Fletcher and Fang eating _____ in outer space. (Outer Space)

6. Jill always tapped on her _____. (All books)

7. Someone wrecked the sand _____ that Jill and Gwen built. (Vacation)

Down

1. Gwen and Jill loved to _____ mysteries (All books.)

2. A _____ had been stolen from Jill's living room. (Birthday Party)

3. _____ was the name of Jill's dog. (All books)

4. Someone put _____ into the lemonade. (Lemonade Stand)

5. Mr. _____ haunted the school. (Haunted School)

6. Fletcher was a _____ dog. (All books)

Something is going on
Print the circled letters here. _____

What do they spell? ___ ___ ___ ___ ___ ___ ___ ___ ___ ___ ___

You're Invited!

Henry Reed's Birthday Party!

Based on the books by Keith Robertson

Celebrate Henry's 12th Birthday: Program (60–40 minutes)

Story: *Henry Reed Inc.* Read excerpts from the book.

Project: **Invent It** (Instructions on p. 111)

Story: *Henry Reed's Journey* Tell this story.

Activity: **Take a Journey** (Instructions on p. 112)

Booktalks: Tell about one incident from each of the other Henry Reed books. Do not reveal the ending. Encourage the children to read the books to discover how each situation is resolved.

Project: **Make and Keep a Journal** (Instructions on p. 111)

Snacks: Light the candles on the cake, and sing "Happy Birthday" to Henry Reed. Blow out the candles and make a wish. Bring each child a piece of cake and a cup of juice.

Story Bags: Give the children their story bags as they leave.

I've been to Henry Reed's birthday party at:

Planning and Promotion

Advertising Display: Have a suitcase with a poster attached to the front. Print the program and registration information on the poster. Have suitcase-shaped flyers with the program and registration information for people to take.

Room Decorations: Decorate the room to look like Henry's room. Use articles from the stories.

Name Tags: Use any self-stick birthday name tags you choose.

Snacks: Have a birthday cake with a picture of one of Henry's inventions on it. Write "Happy Birthday, Henry" on it. Insert twelve candles. Serve juice for beverage.

Story Bags: Give each child a brown lunch sack with a sign attached that says, I'VE BEEN TO HENRY REED'S BIRTHDAY PARTY AT _____. The children can use the bags to carry home their projects, the prize they win playing the game on page 111-112, a bookmark listing the Henry Reed materials available in your library and the puzzle on page 113. Party prizes can include pencils and anything related to the Henry Reed stories.

Henry Reed books by Keith Robertson

Books are listed in series order.

Henry Reed Inc. New York: Viking, 1958. Henry is spending the summer with his aunt and uncle. He and his neighbor Midge decide to set up their own business.

Henry Reed's Babysitting Service. New York: Viking, 1966. Henry and Midge set up a baby-sitting service. They are amazed at how hard it is to take care of little kids.

Henry Reed's Journey. New York: Viking, 1966. Henry and Midge's family travel from San Francisco to New Jersey. Along the way they stop in Yosemite, the Grand Canyon and many other exciting places.

Henry Reed's Big Show. New York: Viking, 1970. Henry and Midge have some grand ideas for a big show. It turns out to be a rodeo.

Henry Reed's Think Tank. New York: Viking, 1986. Henry and Midge are back in business solving problems for people.

Instructions for Invent It

Materials
construction paper (white and colored)

paper tubes, tin foil, wrapping paper, yarn, fabric scraps, cardboard boxes, glitter, pom-poms, etc.

scissors

glue

notebook paper

pencils & crayons

Directions
1. Tell the children they are to use the materials to invent something no one else has invented.

2. Then they can use the notebook paper and pencils to write about their invention.

3. Let the children take turns showing and telling about their inventions.

4. Display these for awhile and then let the children take them home.

Ideas: A trap for catching siblings, teachers, parents, etc.; A computer that does your homework without even being told to; A room cleaning machine, etc.

Instructions for Make and Keep a Journal

Materials
crayons

paper punch

laminating film and machine or clear contact paper

Items below are required for each child

2 sheets of 9"x12" colored construction paper

20 sheets of notebook paper

3 fasteners

pencil   *This is one of the party prizes.*

> *Hint: Have a few extra of each item on hand, just in case something gets lost.*

Directions
1. Tell children they are going to make and begin to keep journals.

2. Give each child two sheets of construction paper and let them decorate the covers. Remind them to print their names on the front cover.

3. Laminate covers.

4. Punch three holes in each set of covers, add notebook paper, and attach fasteners. Children can add more sheets of paper if necessary.

5. Tell the children to write the current day's date (month, date and year) on the first page. Give them a few minutes to write a journal entry. They can draw pictures, too.

6. Encourage them to write in their journals daily. If at school, give them time during the day to write in their journals. If doing this in libraries, let them take their journals home to use.

Instructions for Take a Journey

Materials

1 large wall map of the United States. *Laminate or cover with clear contact paper.*

push pins

prizes *Anything state related: decals, magnets etc.*

blindfold

Prior to the program

1. Make sure there are books on the shelf for each of the states.

2. Hide one prize among each state. You will need 50 prizes. You probably will not need all 50, but there is no way of knowing which states will be "visited" until the game is played. Hide well, between books, under the shelf, etc.

3. Put the map on the wall at child height.

Directions

1. Blindfold each child. Give child a push pin. Turn child around three times and point the child in the direction of the map. Have the child put a push pin in map.

2. They will have landed in a state. Children should go to the catalog, look up the call number, write it down and go find a state book and the prize hidden nearby.

3. Only one "visitor" per state is allowed. If a child lands on a state that has already been visited, they must try again.

   Idea: This can be the start of doing "State Reports."

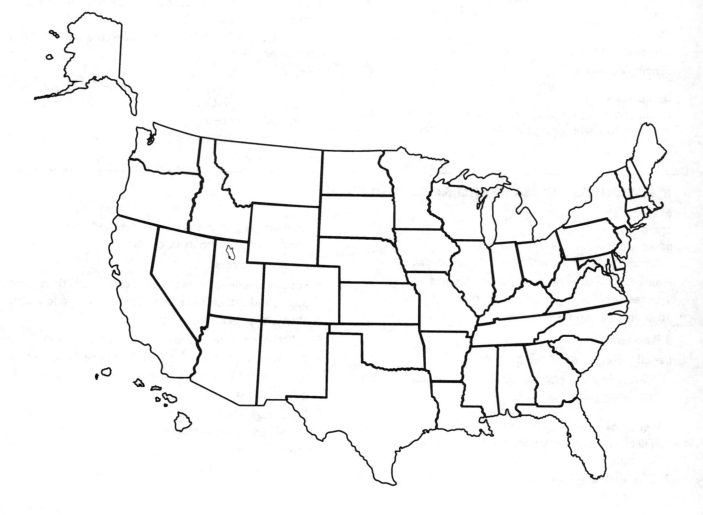

Reading Henry's Journal

You are going to have to look in the Henry Reed books to find the answers to this puzzle.

1. Henry named the dog he found ___ ◯ ___ ___ ___ . *(Henry Reed, Inc.)*

2. Henry and ___ ___ ___ ___ ◯ decided to go into the ◯ ___ ___ ___ ___ ◯ ___ ___ business. *(Henry Reed, Inc.)*

3. ___ ___ ___ ___ ___ ___ ___ Osborn liked to ___ ___ ___ ___ from Henry when he took care of her. *(Henry Reed's Baby Sitting Service)*

4. Hannah Haskell gave ___ ___ ◯ ___ to Henry and Midge as a reward for rescuing him on Fisherman's Wharf. *(Henry Reed's Journey)*

5. While visiting the ___ ◯ ___ ___ ___ ___ ◯ ___ ___ ___ ___ ___ Midge dropped the car keys over the edge. *(Henry Reed's Journey)*

6. Midge's horse was named ___ ___ ___ ___ ___ ___ ___. *(Henry Reed's Big Show)*

7. Henry and Midge decided to have a ◯ ___ ___ ___ ___ . *(Henry Reed's Big Show)*

8. Henry's father worked for the diplomatic ___ ___ ___ ◯ ___ ___ ___ . *(All books)*

9. Henry and Midge went to the shopping center where they took a poll on kid's ___ ___ ___ ◯ ___ ___ ___ ___ ___ ___ . *(Henry Reed's Think Tank)*

10. Henry and Midge wanted to have a ___ ___ ___ ◯ flying ___ ___ ___ ◯ ___ ___ ◯ ___ . *(Henry Reed's Think Tank)*

Unscramble the circled letters to spell

___ ___ ___ ___ ___ ___ ___ ___   ___ ___ ___ ___ ___ ___

You know the rest.   ___ ___ ___   ___ ___ ___ ___ ___

(All books)

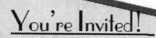

Matthew Martin's Birthday Party!

Based on the books by Paula Danziger

Celebrate Matthew's 11th Birthday: Program (60–90 minutes)

Story: *Everyone Else's Parents Said Yes* Tell this story.

Project: **Make Monster Cards** (Instructions on p. 116)

Booktalks: Highlight the other Matthew stories in the series. Tell about one incident in each book. However, do not reveal the ending. Encourage the children to read the books to see how the situation was resolved.

Game: **Fishing for Prizes** (Instructions on p. 115)

Project: **The Biggest Birthday Card Ever** (Instructions on p. 115)

Snacks: Light the candles on the cake and sing "Happy Birthday" to Matthew. Blow out the candles and make a wish. Bring each child a piece of birthday cake, a cup of chocolate milk shake and a scoop of chocolate ice cream.

Story Bags: Give each child a story bag. Make sure their monster cards and the prize they won are inside.

I've been to Matthew Martin's birthday party at:

Planning and Promotion

Advertising Display: Make a poster that has birthday lists similar to the ones that Matthew makes for his party in the book *Everyone Else's Parents Said Yes*. Include a list of activities: Storytelling, Games, Prizes, Food, Fun. Have a list of foods: Cake, Ice Cream, Milk Shakes. Include the program and registration information on the flyer. Provide flyers with the program and registration information for people to take as reminders.

Room Decorations: Have stars with 11s in them, balloons, birthday banners and streamers. Try to find computer themed table cloth, plates, napkins and cups.

Name Tags: Try to find a computer related self-stick name tag.

Snacks: Have a chocolate birthday cake with chocolate frosting and chocolate ice cream. Use decorating gels in any color to write **HAPPY BIRTHDAY, MATTHEW** on the cake. Decorate it with gummy worms. Have chocolate milk shakes for the beverage.

Story Bags: Give each child a brown paper lunch sack with a sign attached that says, **I'VE BEEN TO MATTHEW MARTIN'S BIRTHDAY PARTY AT** _____ . Inside each bag include, a bookmark with a list of the Matthew Martin books owned by your library, the puzzle on p. 117 and the prize won in the game on p. 115. Party prizes can include the things Matthew gave out: candy, raisins, wax teeth and baseball cards with bubble gum.

Matthew Martin books by Paula Danziger

Books are listed in series order.

Everyone Else's Parents Said Yes. New York: Delacorte Press, 1989. Matthew is planning his 11th birthday party, when he learns that a group of girls are out to "get him."

Make Like a Tree and Leave. New York: Delacorte Press, 1990. Matthew is the cause of an awful lot of trouble, including getting his friend Brian trapped inside a homemade mummy cast.

Earth to Matthew. New York: Delacorte Press, 1991. Matthew takes an interest in the environment when his class begins to study ecology.

Not for a Billion Gazillion Dollars. New York: Delacorte Press, 1992. Matthew needs to earn money to pay off his debts to his classmates and buy a new computer program.

Instructions for Fishing for Prizes

Materials
5 chairs with rungs across the back

5 ten foot pieces of yarn

1 colorful fish per child *On the fish will be a clue to help them find their prize.*

1 prize per child *(candy, wax teeth, baseball cards.)*

paper punch

Prior to the program
1. On the back of each fish, write a clue to help the players find the hidden party prizes. Every clue will tell the children to look something up in the catalog. The call number will be where their prize is located. You will need one location per child. Make each one different. (Look up DOGS. Write down the number. Look there for your prize. Other locations: BASEBALL, ANTS, SPIDERS, WHALES, ILLINOIS, FRANCE, etc.)
2. Hide the prizes in the correct locations. Keep a master list of locations.
3. Attach one end of each string to the back of a chair.
4. Punch a small hole in each fish.
5. Add one fish to each line and put it close to the chair.

Directions
1. Set up the chairs across the back of the area.
2. Have children stand about 9' away from the chairs.
3. Give each child the end of a fishing line. They must try to jiggle the fish so it comes to them. *They May Not Lower The Line And Let It Slide. And They Can Only Use One Hand.* The other hand must be kept behind their backs.
4. As soon as a child "catches" as fish, they remove it and follow the instructions on it.
5. Attach a new fish to each line as a fish is caught and let the next children "fish."
6. Keep playing until everyone has had a turn. All children are winners.

Biggest Birthday Card Ever

Materials
1 12" x 18" piece of construction paper per child *(Use a variety of colors.)*

crayons and markers

tape

Directions
1. Give each child a piece of paper.
2. Tell them to keep it flat and in a horizontal position.
3. Have them design a large birthday card for Matthew. It can be funny and silly.
4. Tell them to write a greeting and sign their name.
5. Lay all of the cards face down. Make sure they are all right side up, so that when the large card is turned over, nothing will be upside down.. Tape them together along the seams on the back.
6. Turn the card over to display "the biggest birthday card ever."
7. Send the card to author, Paula Danziger with a note telling her how much the children enjoyed getting acquainted with Matthew.

Alternative: Display the card for all to see and enjoy.

Instructions for Making Monster Cards

Materials
5 pieces of white cover or card stock paper per child
  Use pattern below. Copy on both sides of paper.
crayons and markers

Directions
1. Give each child the five pieces of paper and coloring supplies.

2. Tell the children they are to create five original monsters. Make one card for each monster. On the front of the card, draw the monster. Answer the questions about the monster on the back.

3. Children may take these home. Perhaps they can arrange a time to trade with one another.

front

Sample monster cards

MONSTER: _____

WEIGHT _____

HEIGHT _____

DESCRIPTION _____
_____
_____

EATS: _____
_____

LIVES IN: _____

BEHAVIORIAL CHARACTERISTICS
_____
_____

back

Something to solve

Look on the shelves to find books with these numbers. When you find out which subjects they are, write them in the spaces provided. Unscramble the circled letters to spell _____.
Who is this? _____

567.1   ◯ __ __ __ __ __ __ __

976.7   __ __ __ __ __ ◯ __

636.8   __ ◯ __ __

976.1   __ __ __ __ __ ◯ __

796.44   __ __ ◯ __ __ __ __ __ __

796.342 __ __ __ ◯ __ __ __

983   __ __ ◯ __ __

599.5   __ __ ◯ __ __ __

974.1   ◯ __ __ __ __

625.1   __ __ __ ◯ __

941.1   __ __ __ ◯ __ __ __

799.32   __ __ __ __ ◯ __

You're Invited!

Millie Cooper's Birthday Party!

Based on the books by Charlotte Herman

Celebrate Millie's 8th Birthday: Program (60–90 minutes)

Story: *Millie Cooper, 3B* Tell this story to the children.

Activity: **I Am Special** (Instructions on p. 119)

Story: *Millie Cooper, Take a Chance* Read the chapter, "Valentine's Day."

Project: **Make a Valentine for Millie** (Instructions on p. 120)

Booktalks: Choose several incidents from the other Millie Cooper books and relate them to the children. However, do not tell how the situations are resolved. Encourage the children to read the books to discover how Millie settles each situation.

Game: **Bean Bag Scramble** (Instructions on p. 120)

Snacks: Light the candles on the cake, and sing "Happy Birthday" to Millie. Make a wish and blow out the candles. Bring each child a piece of cake, some ice cream and a cup of juice.

Story Bags: Give children their story bags as they leave. Make sure their "I Am Special" project and their prize from Bean Bag Scramble are inside.

I've been to Millie Cooper's birthday party at:

Planning and Promotion

Advertising Display: Make a large cutout of Millie Cooper. Have her holding a sign with the program and registration information on it. Provide colorful flyers with the program and registration information for people to take as reminders.

Room Decorations: Decorate the room for a birthday party. Have balloons, **HAPPY BIRTHDAY, MILLIE COOPER** banners and streamers. Choose any birthday-themed tablecloth, paper plates, cups and napkins.

Name Tags: Have any self-stick birthday name tags.

Snacks: Have a pink cake with pink frosting. Decorate the cake with red and pink hearts. Print

"Happy Birthday, Millie Cooper" on it. Insert eight candles. Have pink ice cream. Serve cranberry juice for the beverage.

Camera and film: Have an instant camera loaded so that you can take a picture of each child arriving. Print the child's name on the back. These photos will be used for the "I Am Special" project on p. 119.

Story Bags: Use colorful paper lunch sacks. Attach a sign that says: **I'VE BEEN TO MILLIE COOPER'S BIRTHDAY PARTY AT** _____ . Label each bag with a child's name. Party prizes can include: a neat pen with drawings on it, an unusual eraser, the prize the children win playing the Bean Bag Scramble on p. 120 , the "I Am Special" project on p. 119, a bookmark listing the Millie Cooper materials available in your library and the puzzle on p. 121.

Millie Cooper books by Charlotte Herman

Books are listed in series order.

Millie Cooper, 3B. New York: E.P. Dutton, 1985. When Millie struggles with the challenges of third grade, she learns that she is a very special person.

Millie Cooper, Take a Chance. New York: E.P. Dutton, 1988. Millie learns to take chances when the enters a contest.

Millie Cooper and Friends. New York: E.P. Dutton, 1995. Now in fourth grade, Millie is afraid she will lose her best friend when a new girl moves in.

Instructions for I Am Special

Materials
1 12" x 18" sheet of pastel-colored construction paper per child

1 sheet of notebook paper per child

several sharpened pencils per child

crayons

instant photo of each child taken upon arrival

glue sticks

Prior to the program
Fold each piece of construction paper in half horizontally, so it looks like a book cover.

Directions
Do this as a group, one step at a time.

1. Give each child a piece of notebook paper and a pencil.

2. Tell the children to write down things that make them special. (I am a good singer. I am creative. I love animals.)

3. Give each child a colored cover. Tell them to open it and draw pictures on the left-hand side of the paper. Have them glue their notebook paper to the right-hand side.

4. Give children their photos. Have them glue photos to the front cover. Tell them to write the words **I Am Special** on their covers. Have them trace their hand on the back cover. They can color it.

5. Have them put their names on their folders.

6. Put each child's folder into his/her story bag.

   Hints: Assist children as needed with writing and spelling.

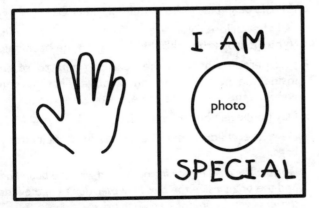

I Am Special cover

I Am Special interior pages

Instructions for Make a Valentine for Millie

Materials

various shades of red and pink construction paper

red and pink crayons and markers

red and pink glitter

glue

scissors

Directions

1. Let the children use paper, crayons, makers and glitter to create a Valentine for Millie.

2. Encourage children to be creative. Make the Valentines three dimensional, e.g., animals, flowers etc.

3. Send the Valentine's to Millie in care of author Charlotte Herman. Include a letter telling about the party you had for Millie. If she responds, display her letter along with the photos you took of the program.

Alternatives: Display the Valentine's the children made. Children can take their Valentine's home.

Hints: You might need to show the children how to fold the paper in half and cut out a heart

Show them out to cut the center out of a heart to make two hearts.

Show them how to make Valentine flowers, animals, and three dimensional

Instructions for Bean Bag Scramble

Materials

1 beanbag

audiocassette player and tape of birthday music

masking tape

1 prize per child *(Try to find a variety of prizes: tops, magnets, jumbo chalk, small plastic animals, etc.)*

1 large box with a separate top.

tissue paper

ribbon.

birthday wrapping paper

Prior to the program

1. Wrap the top and bottom of the box separately.

2. Cut a hole large enough to fit a hand inside in the top of the box.

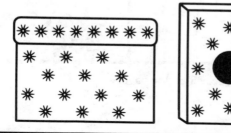

3. Wrap each prize in tissue paper and tie with ribbon.

4. Put the party prizes into the box.

5. Put the lid on the box.

6. Tape a circle on the floor.

Directions

1. Have the children stand around the circle.

2. Put the bean bag in the middle of the circle.

3. Tell the children you are going to play the music. When it stops they should try to grab the bean bag.

4. The person who gets the bean bag gets to reach inside the box and pull out a prize. That person watches the rest of the game.

5. Play until everyone wins a prize.

6. Have the children put the prizes into their story bags.

Bonus: The child remaining at the end wins the bean bag and the prize inside the box. However, don't tell the kids this until you award the bean bag prize.

Hint: Remind the children that everyone will win a prize. They don't need to fight over the beanbag. Tell them to play carefully so that no one gets hurt.

Puzzling

Fill in the missing letters to complete the names of some of the characters in the Millie Cooper books. When you are finished the letters in the vertical box will spell something special from one of the stories. What is this?

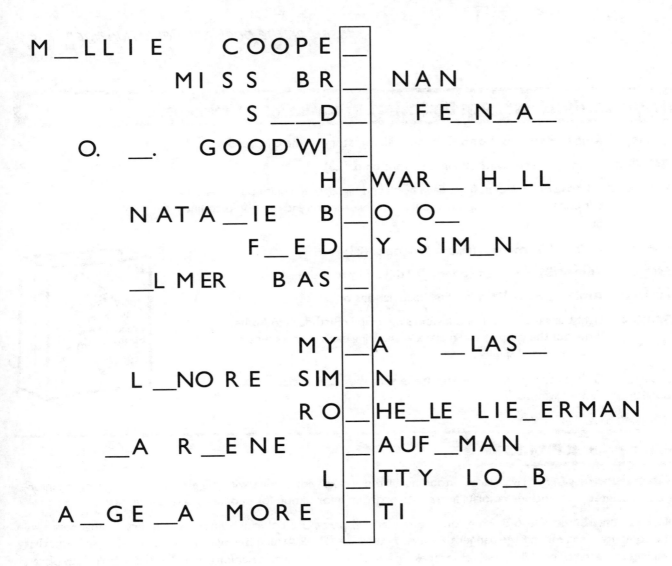

M _ L L I E   C O O P E _ _

MISS   BR _ _ NAN

S _ _ D _   FE _ N _ A _

O. _ .   GOODWI _

H _ WAR _   H _ LL

NAT A _ IE   B _ O O _

F _ E D _ Y   SIM _ N

_ L MER   B A S _

MY _ A   _ LAS _

L _ NO R E   SIM _ N

RO _ HE _ LE   LIE _ ERMAN

_ A R _ E N E   _ AUF _ MAN

L _ TT Y   LO _ B

A _ GE _ A   MORE _ TI

Letty Loeb   Miss Brennan   Myra Glass
Sandy Feinman   Angela Moretti   Freddy Simon
Millie Cooper   Howard Hall   Elmer Bass
Lenore Simon   Rochelle Lieberman   Natalie Bloom
O.J. Goodwin   Marlene Kauffman

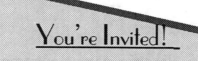

You're Invited!

Amber Brown's
Birthday Party!

Based on the books by Paula Danziger

Celebrate Amber's 9th Birthday: Program (60–90 minutes)

Story: *Amber Brown Is Not a Crayon* Tell this story to the children.

Activity: **Decorate the Banner** (Instructions on p. 123)

Booktalks: Choose one incident from each book and highlight it. Tell it up to the climax, but don't tell the ending. Encourage the children to read the books to find out how the stories end.

Game: **Colorful Surprises** (Instructions on p. 123)

Story: *Amber Brown Goes Fourth* Tell this story to the children.

Project: **Amber Brown Windsocks** (Instructions on p. 124)

Snacks: Light the candles on the cake and sing "Happy Birthday" to Amber. Blow out the candles and make a wish. Bring each child a piece of cake and a cup of juice.

Story Bags: Give children their story bags. Make sure they have their Amber windsocks.

I've been to Amber Brown's birthday party at:

Planning and Promotion

Advertising Display: Have a large cutout of a birthday cake with candles with the program and registration information printed on it. Include colorful flyers with program information for people to take as reminders.

Room Decorations: Decorate the room for a birthday party. Use colorful balloons, streamers and banners. Use the computer to create a large banner that says, **HAPPY BIRTHDAY, AMBER BROWN**. Use white paper. Use a font that outlines the letters. The children will color these in later. Try to find crayon or color-themed birthday tablecloth, plates, cups and napkins.

Name Tags: Use the crayon name tags on p. 124 in a variety of colors.

Snacks: Have Amber Brownies with chocolate frosting. Decorate the frosting with a variety of candies. Write Happy Birthday, Amber on the brownies. Have hot chocolate for the beverage.

Story Bags: Give each child a white lunch sack. Attach a crayon-shape (p. 124) with the words **I'VE BEEN TO AMBER BROWN'S BIRTHDAY PARTY AT** _____ printed on it. Children can use the bag to carry home the prize they win playing the game on p. 123, a crayon-shaped bookmark listing the Amber Brown materials available in your library and the puzzle on p. 125. Party prizes can include: Happy Birthday pencils and a brown crayon.

Amber Brown books by Paula Danziger

Books are listed in series order.

Amber Brown Is Not a Crayon. New York: Putnam, 1995. Amber and her best friend Justin have a bad fight. Then, Justin moves away!

You Can't Eat Your Chicken Pox, Amber Brown. New York: Putnam, 1995. Amber Brown comes down with chicken pox while on vacation in London.

Amber Brown Goes Fourth. New York: Putnam, 1995. Can Amber Brown find a new best friend?

Amber Brown Wants Extra Credit. New York: Putnam, 1996. Amber is not thrilled when she finds out she has to meet her mother's boyfriend Max. She really wants her dad to come back.

Forever, Amber Brown. New York: Putnam, 1996. Amber's life is still filled with changes, but at least she gets to go visit her friend Justin.

Amber Brown, Sees Red. New York: Putnam, 1997. Amber is angry about the constant arguing between her divorced parents. She is also concerned about their desire to have joint custody of her.

Instructions for Decorate the Banner

Materials

1 long banner with the words

  Happy Birthday, Amber Brown!

  Do not fill in the letters.

crayons in a variety of bright colors

Directions

1. Lay the banner flat on a table.

2. Let each party guest decorate one letter. If you have extra letters, have a drawing to see who gets to decorate the other letters or decorate them yourself.

3. The children can add greetings and sign their names.

4. Send the banner to author Paula Danziger with a letter telling about your party for Amber. If she responds, display her letter along with the photos you took of the program.

Alternative: *Display the banner for all to enjoy.*

Instructions for Colorful Surprises

Materials

1 colored, plastic egg per child

1 party prize per child (whistle, top, ball, pin and other things Amber would give as party prizes. Have a variety of prizes.)

1 large basket to hold the eggs

1 audiocassette of birthday music and a tape player

tissue paper in a variety of colors

ribbon in a variety of colors

Staff members, parents or volunteers to help supervise the Colorful Surprises Game.

Prior to the program

1. Put a clue inside each egg that directs the child to a prize location. Try to have one location per child.

   Examples:

   Paula Danziger writes the Amber Brown books. Look there.

   We have audiocassettes of the Amber stories. Look there.

   Amber likes to read magazines. Look there.

   Amber likes books by Patricia Reilly Giff. Look there.

2. Wrap prizes in tissue paper and tie with ribbons.

3. Hide prizes in the selected, challenging locations.

Directions

1. Have the children sit in a circle.

2. Give one child the basket of eggs.

3. Play the music.

4. Instruct the children to pass the basket around the circle as the music plays.

5. When the music stops, the child holding the basket, removes an egg and leaves the circle. That child opens the egg, silently reads the clue and goes to search for the prize. (Have your helpers on hand in the "searching areas.")

6. Continue until each child has an egg.

7. After the children find their prizes, they return to the room. Put each child's prize into their story bag.

Hint: *If desired, place a balloon sticker in the location where each prize is hidden.*

Instructions for Amber Windsocks

Materials

crayons
pencils
stapler and staples
glue sticks
paper punch

One of each item below per child

1 12" strand of colorful yarn

7 2" colored circles

7 12" long strips of brightly colored crepe
paper (Use a variety of colors.)

1 12" x 18" piece of heavy duty, brightly colored construction paper

1 9" x 12" piece of white construction paper

Prior to the program

1. Curve paper into a tube and staple it
   at the top and bottom.

2. Punch two holes in the top of the tube.

3. Attach and tie the yarn to the top
   of the paper tube.

Directions

Do this as a group, one step at a time.

1. Give each child the white construction paper. Tell
   them to draw, color and, cut out a picture of Amber
   Brown.

2. Give each child a colored tube.

3. Have the children glue the pictures of Amber to the
   tubes.

4. Let each child choose which color streamers to
   use.

5. Glue the streamers to the bottom of the tube.

6. Give each child the six colored circles. Have them
   write one favorite event from each Amber Brown
   story on a circle.

7. Have the children glue one circle to the end of each
   streamer.

8. Have the children write their names on their windsocks. Children may take these home.

Patterns

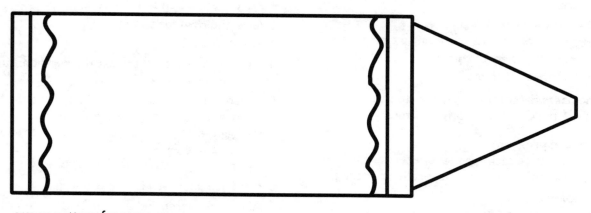

crayon pattern for name tag
and story bag

Happy Birthday Amber Brown

Can you complete these titles?

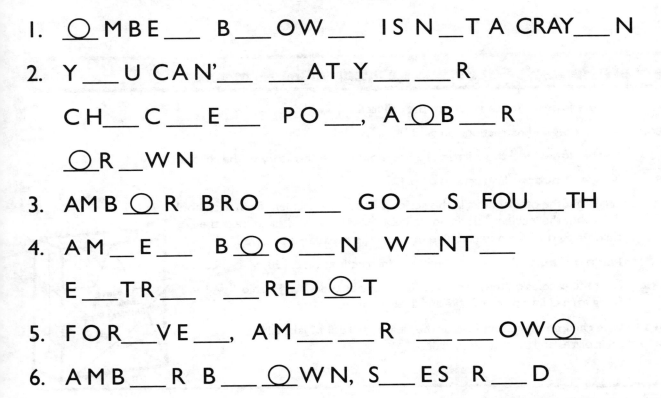

1. (O)MBE___ B___OW___ IS N___T A CRAY___N

2. Y___U CAN'___ ___AT Y_____R CH___C___E___ PO___, A(O)B___R (O)R___WN

3. AMB(O)R BRO_____ GO___S FOU___TH

4. AM___E___ B(O)O___N W___NT___ E___TR___ ___RED(O)T

5. FOR___VE___, AM_____R _____OW(O)

6. AMB___R B___(O)WN, S___ES R___D

Print the circled letters in the spaces below.

___ ___ ___ ___ ___ ___ ___ ___ ___ ___

What's special about this word? _____

You're Invited!

Herbie Jones' Birthday Party!

Based on the books by Suzy Kline

Celebrate Herbie's 9th Birthday: Program (60–90 minutes)

Story: *Herbie Jones* Tell this story to the children.

Project: **Make a Sign** (Instructions on p. 127)

Story: *Herbie Jones and the Birthday Showdown* Tell this story to the children.

Game: **Target Practice** (Instructions on p. 127)

Booktalks: Highlight the other books in this series. Choose one incident from each book. Tell about the incident, but do not tell how it was resolved. Encourage the children to read the books to find out how the situation is resolved.

Project: **Make Birthday Cards for Herbie** (Instructions on p. 128)

Snacks: Light the candles on the cake, and sing "Happy Birthday" to Herbie. Bring each child a piece of cake and a cup of juice.

Story Bags: Give children their story bags as they leave the room. Make sure their prizes and projects are inside.

Planning and Promotion

Advertising Display: Use a large piece of poster board to make an very large birthday invitation. Cut it in half and join the two pieces together with book tape. Print **YOU'RE INVITED TO HERBIE JONES' BIRTHDAY PARTY!** on the front. Decorate it with a western theme. Decorate the inside to look like an invitation too. Have the program and registration information here. Attach this to a large piece of brightly colored poster board. Provide folded flyers made to look like birthday party invitations for people to take as reminders.

Room Decorations: Decorate the room for a birthday party. Use a western theme. Have balloons, streamers and "Happy Birthday, Herbie Jones" banners. Have cowboy hats and other western artifacts.

Name Tags: Choose any self-stick birthday name tag that has a western theme.

Snacks: Have a yellow sheet cake decorated white frosting. Draw something western on it. Print "Happy Birthday, Herbie Jones" on the cake. Serve "western punch" for beverages. (Mix cranberry and orange juice together.)

Story Bags: Use any brightly colored or print lunch sacks. Add a sign that says, **I'VE BEEN TO HERBIE JONES' BIRTHDAY PARTY AT** _____ to the front. Children will use the sacks to carry home their projects, the prize they win playing the game on p. 127, the puzzle on p. 129 and a bookmark listing the Herbie Jones materials available in your library. Party prizes can include: plastic spiders, dog stickers and other western things.

Herbie Jones books by Suzy Kline

Books are listed in series order.

Herbie Jones. New York: Putnam, 1985. Herbie Jones, a third grader, overcomes the challenges of reading and spelling.

What's the Matter, Herbie Jones? New York: Putnam, 1986. Ray can't figure out why Herbie would rather go to the library than spend time having fun with him.

Herbie Jones and the Class Gift. New York: Putnam, 1987. When Herbie and Ray break the class gift for their teacher, they try to replace it.

Herbie Jones and the Monster Ball. New York: Putnam, 1988. Herbie's uncle comes for a visit and decides to coach the baseball team.

Herbie Jones and Hamburger Head. New York: Putnam, 1989. Herbie and his dog help stop a bank robbery.

Herbie Jones and the Dark Attic. New York: Putnam, 1992. Herbie is afraid to sleep in the attic.

Herbie Jones and the Birthday Showdown. New York: Putnam, 1993. Herbie's two friends have their birthday parties on the same day. Whose party should he go to?

Instructions for Make a Sign

Materials
crayons and markers
glue

One of each item below per child
1 piece of 12" x 18" white construction paper
1 piece of 12" x 18" poster board *(optional)*
1 paint stick

Directions
   Do this as a group, one step at a time.
1. Give each child a piece of paper. Tell them to design a sign. It can be any kind of sign they choose to make. *(Happy Birthday sign, a sign that advertises a book, it can advertise an upcoming event, etc.)* An alternative is for you to choose a topic to highlight *(safety, a unit of study, travel poster, etc.)*

2. If you choose, the children can glue their signs to the poster board. That will make them sturdier.

3. Glue the signs to the paint sticks. Have each child print their name on the paint stick.

4. Display these or let the children take them home.

Instructions for Target Practice

Materials
5 squirt guns
watering cans filled with water *(need narrow spout)*
plastic sheets for the floor and wall
target *(make one similar to an archery target)*
1 prize per child *(Have a variety of different prizes.)*
4 cowboy hats
masking tape
tape of western music and audiocassette player

Prior to the program
1. Fill the squirt guns with water. Fill the watering cans with water.
2. Lay the plastic sheets on the floor in front of the wall.
3. Tape a plastic sheet to the wall.
4. Tape the target in the center of the plastic sheet.

5. Tape a line to the floor about 3' from the target.
6. Label each hat with a color that matches the target (blue, yellow, red, black)

Directions
1. One at a time, each child will have a turn to shoot at the target.
2. Have the child face the target and aim the gun. Try to hit one of the colored circles with the water.
3. When a child hits the target, that child gets to reach inside a color-coded hat and pull out a prize. Have them put the prizes into their story bags.
4. Play until everyone has a prize. Everyone is a winner!
   Alternative: Play the game with bean bags rather than squirt guns.

Instructions for Making Birthday Cards

Materials

crayons

1 large mailing envelope and stamps

One of each item below per child

1 12" x 18" piece of colored construction paper

2 pieces of notebook paper

1 pencil with an eraser

Directions

Do this as a group, one step at a time.

1. Give each child the notebook paper. Have them write their favorite incident from one of the Herbie books. Encourage them to tell why they like it.

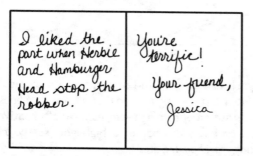

Remind them to put their names on the paper.

2. Give each child a piece of colored construction paper. Have them fold it in half horizontally. Tell them to dec-orate the front like a birthday card. They can draw on the right side inside their card. Have them sign their names.

back cover   front cover

3. Have the children use glue sticks to attach their notebook paper inside the card.

4. Children may decorate the back of their cards if they choose.

5. Gather the cards and put them into the large enve-lope. Send them to author Suzy Kline (through her publisher, Putnam) with a note telling about your program. If she responds, mount her letter on a piece of poster board along with the photos you took of the program. Display it for all to see.

Alternative: *Display the cards for all to enjoy. Let the chil-dren take them home.*

Patterns

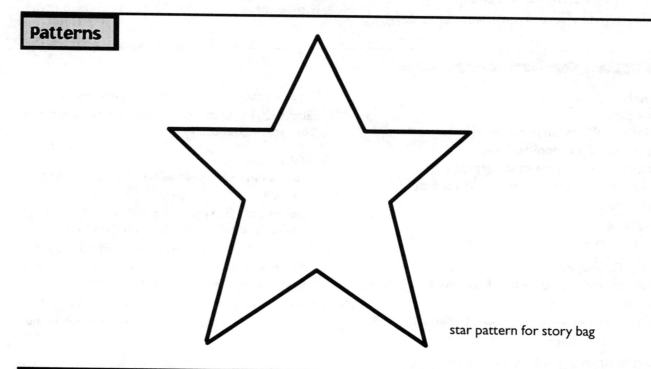

star pattern for story bag

Who's This?

Use this chart to decode the character names below.
Print the circled letters in the spaces to the left.

1=A	6=F	11=K	16=P	21=U	26=Z
2=B	7=G	12=L	17=Q	22=V	
3=C	8=H	13=M	18=R	23=W	
4=D	9=I	14=N	19=S	24=X	
5=E	10=J	15=O	20=T	25=Y	

___ 1. ___ Ⓞ ___ ___ ___ ___ ___
      18 1 25 13 15 14 4

___ 2. ___ ___ ___ ___   ___ ___ Ⓞ ___ ___ ___ ___
      13 9 19 19   16 9 14 11 8 1 13

___ 3. ___ ___ ___ Ⓞ
      10 15 8 14

___ 4. ___ Ⓞ ___ ___ ___ ___
      13 1 18 7 9 5

___ 5. ___ ___ Ⓞ ___ ___ ___ ___ ___ ___ ___ ___ ___
      8 1 13 2 21 18 7 5 18 8 5 1 4

___ 6. ___ ___ ___ ___ ___ Ⓞ
      8 5 18 2 9 5

___ 7. ___ Ⓞ ___ ___ ___ ___
      15 12 9 22 9 1

___ 8. ___ ___ ___ Ⓞ ___ ___
      16 8 9 12 9 16

___ 9. ___ ___ . ___ ___ ___ ___ Ⓞ   ___ ___ ___ ___
      13 18   8 15 4 7 5   11 9 19 19

You're Invited!

Laura Ingalls Wilder's Birthday Party!

Based on the books by Laura Ingalls Wilder

Celebrate Laura's 10th Birthday: Program (60–90 minutes)

Story: *Little House in the Big Woods* If Laura is helping with the program, let her tell this story from her point of view. Otherwise tell it yourself.

Project: **Make a Sampler** (Instructions on p. 132)

Booktalks: Choose one incident from each of the books in this series. Tell about the incident right up to the climax. Make sure you don't reveal the outcome. Have the children to read the books to find out how the situation is resolved.

Game: **Gone Fishin'** (Instructions on p. 131)

Songs: Sing these songs that Laura and her family sang: "Yankee Doodle Went to Town," "Pop Goes the Weasel," and "Dixie." If you know someone with a fiddle who can accompany your sing along, all the better.

Story: "Country Party" from **On the Banks of Plum Creek** Let Laura tell this story.

Snacks: Give each child a heart-shaped cake (or cookie) and a cup of juice. Put a candle in Laura's cake, light it and sing "Happy Birthday." Let Laura make a wish and blow out the candle.

Story Bags: Give children their story bags as they leave.
Make sure their party prizes and samplers are inside the bags.

I've been to Laura Ingalls' birthday party at:

Planning and Promotion

Laura was born on Feb. 7 (1867) so you may want to plan your party for February.

Advertising Display: Have a covered wagon with a sign attached giving the program and registration information. Provide wagon-shaped flyers with the program information for people to take as reminders.

Room Decorations: Decorate the room to look like the inside of the Ingalls cabin. Have a rocking chair, braided rug and other artifacts from her lifetime. The staff members presenting the program can dress in period costume. You can also ask the children to come in period costumes.

Guest Character: Have someone dress up and portray Laura as an adult. She can assist with the program.

Name Tags: Use the covered wagon pattern on p. 133.

Snacks: Bake white heart-shaped cupcakes. Provide pink frosting, decorating gels and other cake decorating items. Let children decorate their own cakes. You can substitute heart-shaped cookies for the cakes. Drink cranberry juice.

Story Bags: Make one cloth sack for each child. Use the pattern on p. 133. You can substitute brown, paper lunch sacks. Use marker to print, **I'VE BEEN TO LAURA INGALLS' BIRTHDAY PARTY AT** _____ on each bag. Children will use their sacks to carry home the prize they win playing the game on p. 131, the puzzle on p. 134 and the covered wagon-shaped list of Laura Ingalls materials owned by your library.

Materials and Prep

Books by Laura Ingalls Wilder

Books are listed in series order.

Little House in the Big Woods. New York: Harper & Row, 1932, 1953. Laura and her family live in an isolated cabin in the Wisconsin woods. They eat wild animals that their father shoots. They sing songs and tell stories.

Little House on the Prairie. New York: Harper & Row, 1935, 1953. The Ingalls have moved to a new home. It is in Indian territory where they encounter many dangers.

Farmer Boy. New York: Harper & Row, 1935, 1953. Like other boys his age, Almonzo wants to do a man's work.

On the Banks of Plum Creek. New York: Harper & Row, 1937, 1953. New experiences await the Ingalls family as they settle in Plum Creek. Their house is unlike any other house they have had before. It is underground!

By the Shores of Silver Lake. New York: Harper & Row, 1939, 1953. There is no choice. The Ingalls have to move out west where they face many new challenges. Ma has a baby and Mary becomes ill and goes blind.

The Long Winter. New York: Harper & Row, 1940, 1953. It is one of the worst and most dangerous winters ever. There is one blizzard after another. One blizzard lasts for three long days.

Little Town on the Prairie. New York: Harper & Row, 1941, 1953. The Ingalls family is now living in town. Mary goes away to school, and Laura becomes a teacher.

These Happy Golden Years. New York: Harper & Row, 1943, 1953. Laura has fallen in love. She and Almonzo got married.

The First Four Years. New York: Harper & Row, 1971. Laura and Almonzo face many challenges and tragedies.

Instructions for Gone Fishin'

Materials

1 child's swimming pool

house plants

4 large sticks with rope attached.

4 magnets

self-stick magnet tape

brown wrapping paper

1 prize per child *(bookmarks, tops and other things you can find from the late 1800s)*

Prior to the program

1. Wrap each prize in brown wrapping paper. Attach a selfstick magnet to each prize.

2. Set up the pool. Put the houseplants around it. You can also add rocks.

3. Put the prizes in the bottom of the pool. Make sure the magnets are facing upwards.

4. Attach the string to each stick. Tie it securely. Attach a magnet to the end of the string.

Directions

1. Explain that Laura liked to go fishing. Tell the children they are going to go fishing today.

2. Select four children to stand around the fishing pond. Give each child a fishing rod, and let them fish. The prize they catch is the prize they get to keep. Put the children's prizes into their story bags.

3. Play until each child has won a prize.

Instructions for Making a Sampler

Materials

yarn in a variety of colors (*Ask people to donate left overs from needlepoint projects.*)

colored markers and crayons

book tape

One of each item below per child

needlepoint needle (*Have extras on hand.*)

12" x 6" piece of muslin

11" x 5" piece of cardboard

6" strand of thick yarn

Prior to the program

1. Use a marker to print each child's name on a piece of muslin. Use upper case letters. Leave a one inch seam allowance on all four sides. Let dry overnight.

2. String each needle with a piece of yarn.

Directions

Do this as a group, one step at a time.

1. Give each child the piece of muslin with their name printed on it.

2. Give each child a threaded needle.

3. Show the children how to stitch each letter with the yarn. They may use large stitches to stitch their names.

Let them use a variety of colors if desired. Stitch each letter separately.

4. Show them how to knot the yarn, so it doesn't pull through the fabric.

5. Give each child a piece of cardboard.

6. Show children how to fit the samplers over the cardboard. Have them glue the edges down on the back.

7. Let the children use crayons to decorate the rest of the sampler.

8. Give each child the 6" piece of yarn. Show them how to use tape to attach it to make a loop on the back of their samplers. They will be able to hang their name samplers.

Hints

1. Have extra pre-threaded needies on hand. When a child runs out of yarn, give them a new threaded needle.

2. Some children will be able to re-thread their own needles. Help those who have difficulty.

3. Explain that when people made samplers, they used many different colors of yarn. They can do that also.

Alternative: Have the children use yarn and glue it to the printed letters of their name.

Instruction for Cloth Story Bag

① Cut two muslin or burlap rectangles for each bag.

fold line

④ Run a piece of rope through the slots so the bag can be tied shut.

stitching line

② Fold over 1" and stitch down along the top edge of both pieces of fabric. Do not sew the side openings together.

③ Pin the two pieces together, inside out. Stitch together on three sides using a 1/4" seam allowance. Turn right side out.

Patterns

covered wagon pattern for name tag

Who's Their Friend?

Unscramble the names of the characters from the *Little House* stories, and print them in the correct spaces. Print the circled letters in each name in the spaces to the left.

____ ARYM ◯ __ __ __ __

____ RAGEC __ ◯ __ __ __

____ LINECARO __ __ __ __ __ __ ◯ __

____ SIMS ERDWIL __ __ __ __ __ __ ◯ __ __ __ __ __

_____ LIWLIE ◯ __ __ __ __ __ __

____ RICEAR __ ◯ __ __ __ __

____ ARUAL __ __ __ ◯ __

____ SAIDINN __ ◯ __ __ __ __ __

____ SHARELC __ __ __ __ __ ◯ __

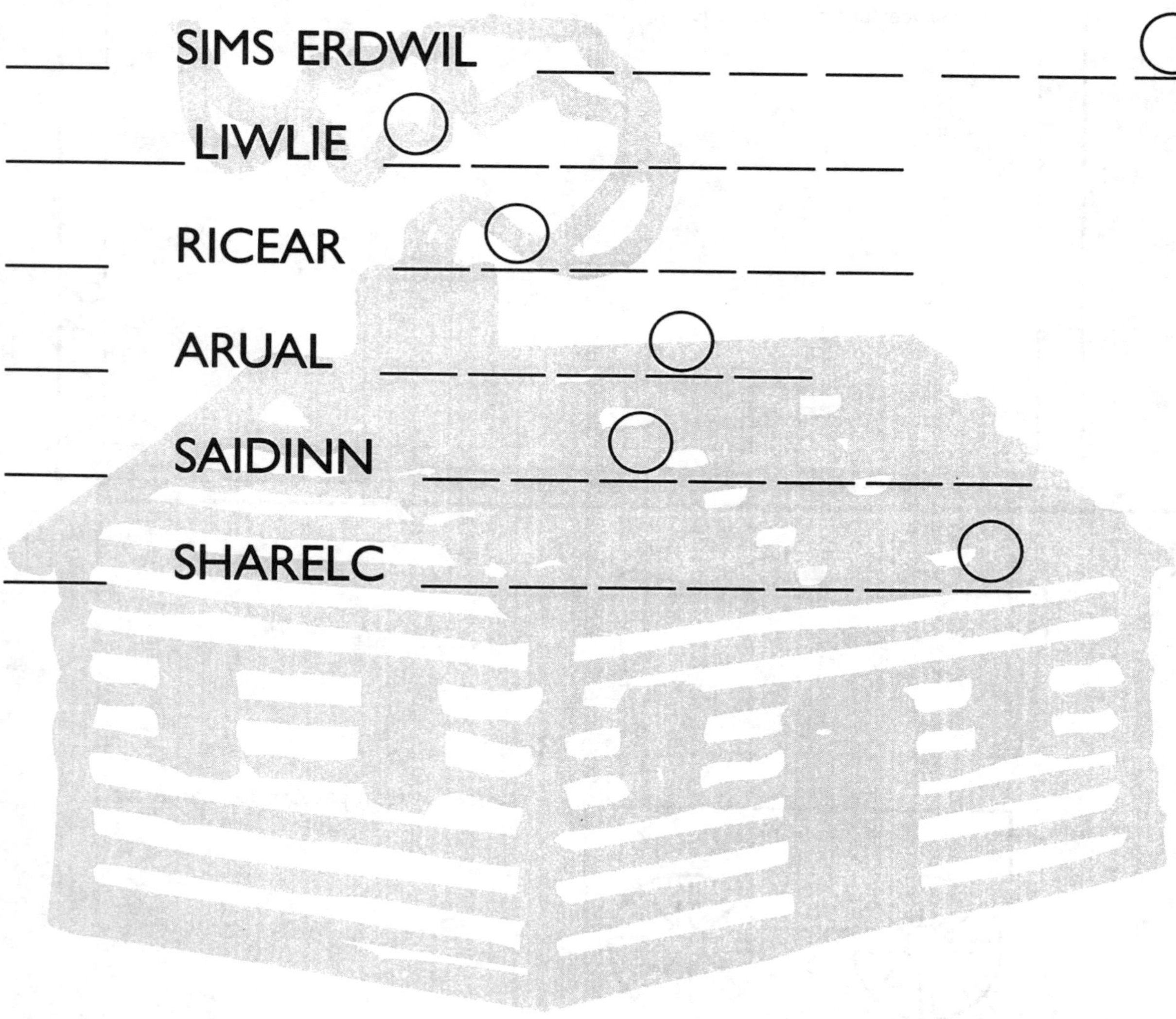

You're Invited!

Cam Jansen's
Birthday Party!

Based on the books by David Adler

Celebrate Cam's 11th Birthday: Program (40 minutes–2 hours)

Story: *Cam Jansen and the Mystery of the Stolen Diamonds* Tell this story to the children

Project: **Making Mysteries** (Instructions on p. 137)

Booktalks: Choose several Cam Jansen books to highlight. Tell the story up to the climax, but don't reveal the outcome. Encourage the children to read the books to find out how the mystery is solved.

Activity: **The Mystery Hunt** (Instructions on p. 137-139)

Story: *Cam Jansen and the Mystery of the Carnival Prize* Tell this story to the children.

Snacks: Light the candle on Cam's cupcake, and sing "Happy Birthday" to her. Bring each detective a cupcake and a cup of juice. When they find the magnifying glass and candies, say, "That's really strange. You were supposed to find those on the Mystery Hunt. I wonder what's going on around here."

Detective Bags: Give each detective their own bag. They can put the magnifying glasses inside.

> I've been to Cam Jansen's birthday party at:

Planning and Promotion

Advertising Display: Have a large cutout of a girl holding a magnifying glass in her hand. Have her next to a "wanted" poster that says, "Cam Jansen wants YOU to come help her solve mysteries at her birthday party!" The magnifying glass should be magnifying the word you. Have the rest of the program and registration information on the poster. Provide magnifying glass-shaped flyers with the program information for people to take as reminders.

Room Decorations: Use mystery decorations and items from the Cam Jansen stories.

Name Tags: Use the badge pattern on p. 138. Cut these out of silver cardboard. Print child's (detective's) name on a white label and attach it to the badge. Use these colors of markers: blue, red, yellow, green, orange, purple. Have five name tags of each color. Name tags will divide the "detectives" into six Detective Divisions. If you have a multiple-age grouping, mix the ages; in a classroom setting, mix children with different abilities.

Snacks: Serve cupcakes with colored candies baked inside. Frost the cupcakes with chocolate frosting and stick a small, plastic magnifying glass in the top of each. Cover the magnifying glass with frosting so it is not easily seen. Put a number 11 in Cam's cupcake. The candies and magnifying glasses are the missing party prizes from the Mystery Hunt.

Camera and film: Have an instant camera loaded with film. Take a photo of each "detective" upon arrival. Put "detective's" photo in the space provided inside the Detective Case Book, p. 140. Alternatives are to ask the children to bring photos or to have them add photos at home.

Planning and Promotion

Detective Bags: Have one brown lunch sack per "detective." Label each bag with the detective's name. Detectives will search for the missing party prizes (pp. 137-139), and put them in their bags. They can put their Detective Case Books and pencils away after they find the prizes. Also include: a bookmark with a detective theme, the puzzle on p. 142 and a list of the Cam Jansen materials in your library. Attach a label that says, **I'VE BEEN TO CAM JANSEN'S BIRTHDAY PARTY AT** _____ to the front of the bag.

Detective Case Books: Each detective will receive a Detective Case Book upon arrival. Instruct detectives to print their name, school and grade inside the book. When creating the front cover (p. 140), color code them to correspond with the name tags/detective badges. Put three copies of p. 141 inside each book. Label front cover with the detectives' first and last names. Put them in alphabetical order.

Height And Weight: Have a measuring ruler and a scale. Measure and weigh each detective. Detectives can write this information in their books. Detectives can help one another with this.

Fingerprinting: After the photo mentioned above has been taken and glued in the Case Book, each detective may be fingerprinted. Begin with the thumb. Roll from left to right while gently pressing on the pad. Next, make the thumb print in the space provided in the Case Book. Do this for the other fingers as well. Use moistened towelettes to wipe off fingers. Set the books aside to dry. You will need several new, black ink stamp pads, several glue sticks and moistened towelettes.

Materials

Cam Jansen books by David Adler

Books are listed in series order.

Cam Jansen and the Mystery of the Stolen Diamonds. New York: Viking, 1980. The alarm at Parker's Jewelry Store has sounded. What has been stolen?

Cam Jansen and the Mystery of the UFO. New York: Viking, 1980. `There are some strange lights in the sky. What could they be?

Cam Jansen and the Mystery of the Dinosaur Bones. New York: Viking, 1981. Cam looks at the big dinosaur. Something is very wrong with it.

Cam Jansen and the Mystery of the Television Dog. New York: Viking, 1981. Cam is convinced the dog they have seen is a hoax.

Cam Jansen and the Mystery of the Gold Coins. New York: Viking, 1982. First Cam's camera is taken. Then it is the gold coins.

Cam Jansen and the Mystery of the Babe Ruth Baseball. New York: Viking, 1982. Cam looks across the playground. In that instant, she knows where the missing baseball is.

Cam Jansen and the Mystery of the Circus Clown. New York: Viking, 1983. Aunt Molly's wallet is missing. How could someone have taken it?

Cam Jansen and the Mystery of the Monster Movie. New York: Viking, 1984. They were watching an exciting film, but they can't watch the end. A reel of film has mysteriously vanished!

Cam Jansen and the Mystery of the Carnival Prize. New York: Viking, 1984. Why are so many people winning the hardest game at the carnival?

Cam Jansen and the Mystery at the Monkey House. New York: Viking, 1985. How in the world does someone take a group of monkeys out of the monkey house?

Cam Jansen and the Mystery of the Stolen Corn Popper. New York: Viking, 1986. Who is stealing shopping bags from the shoppers?

Cam Jansen and the Mystery of Flight 54. New York: Viking, 1989. Someone has disappeared from the airport. Where can she have gone?

Cam Jansen and the Mystery of the Haunted House. New York: Viking, 1992. Who has stolen Aunt Kate's wallet?

Cam Jansen and the Chocolate Fudge Mystery. New York: Viking, 1993. There is something strange about the woman. Cam and Eric set out to find out what is in her bag.

Cam Jansen and the Triceratops Pops. New York: Viking, 1995. How can so many CD's be sold in such a short time? Or have they been stolen?

Cam Jansen and the Ghostly Mystery. New York: Viking, 1996. A ghost has stolen the money. Now all they have to do was find it!

Instructions for Making Mysteries

Materials

white construction paper
lined notebook paper
pencils
crayons

Directions

1. Give each detective the above materials.

2. Challenge the detectives to think of a mystery they would like Cam Jansen to solve. Tell them to draw a picture of it and write about it. "How would you solve the mystery?"

3. If you are doing this in school, this can be a creative writing assignment. Have each class member share their story with the rest of the class. If you are doing this elsewhere, let the children take these home. Put them into the detective bags.

Ideas:

- There were some strange words on the chalk board at school. What were the words? How did they get there?

- On Halloween when two of the children arrived at the class party, no one else was there. What happened to the others?

- It's Thanksgiving. All of the turkeys from the turkey farm have vanished. Will they be found in time for Thanksgiving?

- There was something strange about the new principal at school.

- All of the books on outer space are missing from the library. The computer lists them as "on shelf." Where are they?

- Someone has stolen all of the birthday party supplies for Cam's party. Who did it?

  Alternative: Display the stories in the library for others to enjoy.

Instructions for the Mystery Hunt

Materials

large colored plastic eggs (blue, red, yellow, green, orange and purple—one of each color) *Each egg will have a different message inside.*

basket for the eggs

squares with clue words printed on them. *The sentence they form tells where to find the next clue. These go inside the eggs.*

large stuffed dog, dog dish and 6 large dog biscuits

large colored balloons (blue, red, yellow, green, orange and purple—one of each color) *Each balloon will have a different message inside.*

small pieces of paper with clues. *They go inside the balloons.*

1 piece of yarn per balloon

1 audiocassette tape per group. Put a colored dot on it (blue, red, yellow, green, orange, and purple—one dot per cassette) *Each tape will have a different message recorded on it.*

colored dots (blue, red, yellow, green, orange and purple) *They will be put on the cassettes, dog biscuits and the fiction shelves.*

birthday wrapping paper and a large bow

large box with a separate bottom and lid.

black contact paper

1 puzzle book per child *You can purchase inexpensive ones or create your own.*

1 treasure map per group. *This is a map of where you are having the hunt.*

colored construction paper (blue, green, red, orange, yellow, purple) *Each will have a different message inside. These go on the fiction shelves.)*

colored construction paper (blue, green etc.) to be wrapped around the magazines.

1 pencil and piece of paper per group. The "Division Assistant" will carry this.

1 "Division Assistant" (helper) per group (staff, volunteer, room parent, older youth etc. per group.)

Prior to the program

1. Put one clue inside each colored egg. Put the basket of eggs by the nursery rhyme books (398.8).

2. Put one clue inside each colored balloon. Blow them up and put them at the Youth Reference Desk.

3. Use the audiocassettes to record one clue for each group. Put a colored dot on each cassette, so each team knows which cassette to listen to. Put them by a tape player in the AV section.

4. Wrap six magazines in colored paper. Put them in the magazine area.

Instructions for the Mystery Hunt (cont)

5. Put the dog and the dish of biscuits in the dog area (636.7).

6. Wrap the bottom and top of the box in birthday paper. Wrap each separately. Put the puzzle books inside the box. Put the lid on. Put the bow on the lid. Hide the box in the 793.7 area.

7. Cut out footprints from the black contact paper. Stick them on the floor, so they lead from the 793.7 shelf back to your program area.

9. Write clues on the colored pieces of folded construction paper. Hide these in different areas of the fiction shelves. (blue—Bs, green—Gs, etc.)

10. Put colored dots on the fiction shelves, so each division knows where to look.

11. Write the clues on the colored sheets of paper. Have these sticking out of the fiction shelves, so they are near the colored dot for each division.

12. Make one treasure map for each group. This is a map of the children's library. Put a colored dot on it, so you know which group gets it. Use beige parchment paper. Burn the edges, so it looks authentic. Use red marker to print a large X to indicate where the first clue is hidden. Each team should be directed to a different starting point. (Audio-Visual, Nursery Rhymes, Reference Desk, Magazines, Non-Fiction/Dogs, Fiction Shelves). The final destination for each group is 793.7 (puzzle books).

13. Walk helpers through the route each will take, so they know where to go. Make sure they have a copy of the solutions, so they can offer assistance if needed.

14. Each group will follow a different route. This helps keep the groups spread out. They will all go to the same places, but they will visit them in a different order. That means each clue location will have a different clue. (E.g.: Green Division will start with the egg clue, go to the magazines, go to AV, etc.)

Directions

1. Tell the children to look at the color of ink used on their name tags. All the people in the blue division go to one area of the room, all the people in the green division go to another area of the room, etc. Assign one "Division Assistant" to each division of detectives.

2. Give each "Division Assistant" the proper treasure map. Have them help the detectives decide where to look for the first clue.

3. Before they depart, remind them that "Detectives must work very quietly. Otherwise they risk being discovered." Challenge detectives to see which group can be the quietest. Also, they are to take only the clue that is meant for their team. Do Not Disturb The Other Clues. Look for the color that matches your division color.

4. See the next page for a sample treasure hunt.

5. Adapt this to meet your individual circumstances.

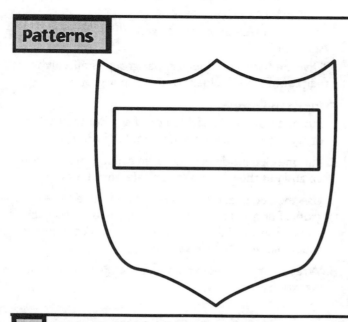

detective badge
Use white labels for the names. Use six different colors of marker (blue, green, yellow, red, orange, purple.) Make five name tags written in each color. This will divide the detectives into "divisions" for the Mystery Hunt. Be sure the color ink on the name tag matches the color of the Case Book.

Sample Mystery Hunt for the Blue Division

Clue 1: The team receives a map with an X marking the spot of the first location. The X is in the audiovisual area. The words: Stop, Look and Listen appear next to the X. When the detectives arrive in the audiovisual area, they choose the tape with the blue dot and listen to it. It says:

Hickety Pickety my black hen.
She lays EGGS now and them.
Sometimes nine, sometimes ten.
Hickety Pickety my black hen.
Where do you think your next clue is hidden? This is a nursery rhyme. Look up Nursery Rhymes in the catalog. What is the Dewey Decimal number for these books?

(Answer: 398.8. The children look here for the next clue.)

Clue 2: There will be a basket of colored eggs in the nursery rhyme area. The sign says:

Take the colored egg that matches your division color. Take it away from here and crack it open.

Inside the egg are squares with words printed on them. The detectives must make a sentence with these words. The sentence says:

These make a loud bang when popped.

The detectives look for the colored balloons. The colored balloons are at the Reference Desk.

Clue 3: The detectives go to the Reference Desk. There they will find the colored balloons. A sign says:

Take the colored balloon that matches your division color. Take it away from here and pop it to get your next clue.

When the balloon is popped, the following message will fall out. It says:

These usually come out once a month. You may have a subscription to one of them. Go there for your next clue.

(Answer: The next clue is in the magazine section.)

Clue 4: The detectives go to the magazines where they will find a magazine rolled up in colored paper. The sign says:

Take the colored wrapper that matches your division color. Open it. Inside is a magazine with a sheet of math problems. Solve these problems, and you will know where to look for your next clue.

$$3 \qquad 6 \qquad 4 \qquad 10$$
$$\underline{+3} \qquad \underline{-3} \qquad \underline{+2} \quad . \quad \underline{-3}$$

(The answer is 636.7)

Clue 5: The detectives will look for 636.7. A stuffed dog will be sitting on the shelf. Next to the dog will be a dish of biscuits. Each biscuit will have a colored dot on it. A sign will say:

Take the biscuit that has a dot matching your division color. Turn it over to discover your next clue location.

Look on the J Fiction Shelves for a blue dot. There will be something else that is blue hidden there.

(The blue dot will appear by the author's names beginning with the letter B. Hidden somewhere among those books will be a blue sheet of paper sticking our from between two books.)

Clue 6: This is the clue:
Unscramble these number words. Print the numeral under each word.

NEVES   INNE   REETH   VENES

____   ____   ____ . ____

(The answer is 793.7)

Clue 7: The detectives go to the 793.7 area where they will find a big box wrapped in birthday paper. The gift tag says,

Open The Box and <u>Take Out One Gift Per Person</u>. Put The Lid Back On The Box. Next Follow The Footprints.

The footprints lead them back to the program area.
Upon returning to the program area:

1. Have detectives put their prizes into their Detective Bags.

2. Have them take their seats.

3. When all have returned, ask them what they found. When they tell you they found a puzzle book say, "That's all? You were also supposed to find some candy and some magnifying glasses. I wonder what went wrong." Send another staff member out to investigate this "strange turn of events." Continue with the next story. The staff member will stay out until you are finished telling the story. Upon return, the staff member will have the plate of cupcakes. He/she can say, "I didn't find the candy or the magnifying glasses, but I did find these cupcakes in the cookbook section. Are you sure you didn't have a clue to go there and look for something? No? That's really strange!" Continue with the snacks. It won't be long before they discover the missing prizes. You can say, "Well, I'm sure glad that mystery is solved!"

Detective

_____'s

(First name) (Last name)

Case Book

Case Book cover Run these in six different colors making sure each "detective" receives a name tag and case book of the same color. This is how you will divide the group into "divisions."

Detective's Name: _____

(First)   (Middle)   (Last)

School: _____ Grade: _____

Eyes: _____   Hair: _____

Weight: _____ lbs. Height: ___ feet ___ inches

Fingerprints--Left Hand				
little finger	ring finger	middle finger	pointer	thumb

Glue your photo in this space

List distinguishing features here: (Missing teeth, freckles, etc)

Fingerprints--Right Hand				
thumb	pointer	middle finger	ring finger	little finger

Detective identification page

Detective's Case Book

Case book recording page: Put three copies of this page in each detective's case book.

Case: _____

Date Started: _____ **Date Solved:** _____

Clues: _____

_____

_____

Suspects: _____

_____

What happened? _____

_____

_____

_____

_____

Case: _____

Date Started: _____ **Date Solved:** _____

Clues: _____

_____

_____

Suspects: _____

_____

What happened? _____

_____

_____

_____

_____

Help Wanted

Cam Jansen's files have been tampered with. She can't find anything. Unscramble each set of words to discover the names of each of the cases she has solved.

MAC SENNAJ DNA EHT YRETSYM FO HET

__ __ __ __ (O) __ __ __ __ __ __   __ __ __   __ __ __

__ __ __ __ __ __ __   __ __   __ __ __

FOU __ __ __

LENSTO DDAIOMNS

__ __ __ __ __ (O) __   __ __ __ __ __ __ __

DSRIAUNO BSEON __ __ __ __ __ __ __ __   __ __ __ (O) __

TERSOMN VIEMO __ __ (O) __ __ __ __   __ __ __ __ __

TLVSOEEIIN ODG __ __ __ __ __ (O) __ __ __   __ __ __

THGILF 45 (O) __ __ __ __ __ __ __

ARNVALCI RPZIE __ __ __ __ __ __ __   __ __ __ __ (O)

EBAB HTUR LLABESAB

__ __ __ __ __ (O)   __ __ __ __   __ __ __ __ __ __ __

LATECHOCO DGFUE

__ __ __ __ __ (O) __ __ __ __   __ __ __ __ __   MYSTERY

KEYMON USEHO __ __ (O) __ __ __   __ __ __ __ __

CUSCIR NWOLC __ __ __ __ __ __   __ __ __ __ __

TOPSACERTRI SPOP

__ __ __ __ __ __ __ __ __ __   __ __ __ (O) __

OLDG OINSC __ __ __ __   __ __ __ __ __

LENSTO NROC PERPOP

__ __ __ __ __ __   __ __ __ __   __ __ (O) __

DEHATUN UOHSE __ __ __ (O) __ __   __ __ __ __ __

STLYGHO SMYTERY

__ __ __ __ __ __ __   __ __ __ __ __ __ __

The first letter in the second word is smudged on the files. Can you figure out what that letter is and write it in the first space of the second word. Then use the circled letters from the puzzle to fill in the rest of the missing letters.

Who is __ __ __ __ __ __ __   __ __ __ __ __ __ __ ?

__ __ __ __ __ __ __ __ __ __ __ __ __ __ __

You're Invited!

Max Malone's Birthday Party!

Based on the books by Charlotte Herman

Celebrate Max's 9th Birthday: Program (60–90 minutes)

Story: *Max Malone and the Great Cereal Rip-Off* Tell this story to the children.

Activity: **Special Offer** (Instructions on p. 144)

Booktalks: Choose some of the other Max Malone books to tell about.
Highlight one incident in each book, however do not reveal the endings.
Encourage the children to read the books to find out how the stories are resolved.

Project: **Superstar Kids** (Instructions on p. 145)

Story: *Max Malone, Superstar* Tell this story to the children.

Game: **Musical Box Tops** (Instructions on p. 144)

Snacks: Light the candles on the cake, and sing "Happy Birthday" to Max. Blow out the candles and make a wish. Bring each child a piece of cake and a cup of astro-juice.

Story Bags: Give the children their story bags as they leave the room.
Make sure their Super Star Kids Cards and prizes are inside.

I've been to Max Malone's birthday party at:

Planning and Promotion

Advertising Display: Have a large poster decorated with balloons, confetti and party hats. Let parts of the party hats and balloons stray from the edges of the poster. Print the program and registration information on the balloons and party hats. Have party hat-shaped flyers with the program information for people to take as reminders.

Room Decorations: Decorate the room for a birthday party using balloons, streamers and banners. Try to find artifacts from the Max Malone stories.

Name Tags: Use the birthday party hat pattern on p. 145.

Snacks: Have a birthday cake frosted with dark blue frosting and planets. Print **HAPPY BIRTHDAY, MAX MALONE** on the cake. Insert nine candles. Serve astro-juice (a mixture of orange and cranberry juice) for the beverage.

Story Bags: Give each child a brown lunch sack that says, **I'VE BEEN TO MAX MALONE'S BIRTHDAY PARTY AT** _____ . The children will use these to carry home the prize they win playing the game, their art project, a bookmark listing the Max Malone materials in your library, and the puzzle on p. 146. Party prizes can include: planet stickers, a magic trick, a baseball card and a small box of cereal.

Max Malone books by Charlotte Herman

Books are listed in series order.

Max Malone and the Great Cereal Rip-off. New York: Henry Holt, 1990. Max Malone sends away for all kinds of free offers from cereal boxes.

Max Malone Makes a Million. New York: Henry Holt, 1991. Max and his friend Gordy find a terrific way to make money.

Max Malone, Superstar. New York: Henry Holt, 1992. Max decides to become Austin's agent and help him become famous doing television commercials.

Max the Magnificent. New York: Henry Holt, 1993. Max is trying to become a magician.

Instructions for Special Offer

Materials

1 piece of 9" x 12" poster board per child
pencils (colored and regular), crayons, markers
glitter
glue
several boxes of various cereals
notebook paper
white construction paper

Directions

1. Give each child a poster board and a regular leaded pencil. Have the other materials readily available.

2. Tell the children to develop a new cereal. What is it called? What is in it? What does it look like? Have them use their notebook paper to write about it.

3. Have the children design a box cover for their new cereal. It must have the name of the cereal and a picture of it. Tell them to use the cereal boxes that are on display for ideas. But, they must create their own original cereal.

4. Now, think of something free that can be offered with the cereal. Tell about it. Draw a picture of it on the poster. Does it need a coupon? If so, design a coupon. Do you have to send away for the free gift? Do you have to save UPC pieces or box tops? Ideas for free things: stickers, sports cards, plastic animals, etc. Encourage the children to think of others.

Instructions for Musical Box Tops Game

Materials

1 cereal box top per child
1 audiocassette of children's songs and tape player
masking tape
1 small prize per child *(plastic bugs and other small inexpensive toys)*
1 bonus prize *(changeable color marker, key chain, etc.)*
1 bucket for the prizes

Prior to the program

1. Cut the front portion off of each cereal box.
2. Put rolled masking tape on the back of each box.
3. Put the prizes into the bucket.

Directions

1. Quickly scatter the boxes on the floor and press them down with your foot so the tape sticks.

2. Tell the children to find a box top to stand on.

3. Explain that when the music is playing they are to walk around the room. When the music stops, they must quickly find a box top to stand on. The first time, everyone will find a box. However, each time after that, a box top will be removed, so that one person will be without a box top to stand on.

4. Play the music. Let the children walk around. Stop the music. Make sure everyone is standing on a box top.

5. Play the music. Stop the music. The child without a box top, gets to reach inside the bucket to pull out a prize.

6. Keep playing until only one child is left. That child gets to choose a prize from the bucket. He/she is also awarded the bonus prize.

Materials and Prep

Instructions for Super Star Kids Cards

Materials

1 6" x 8" piece of white cover stock per child

1 instant camera & film *(An option is to have kids bring school photos, however have the camera and film ready for those who forget.)*

self-stick colored stars

pencils

Directions

1. Give each child one card.

2. Have them fill in the information requested

3. Have the children glue their photos in place.

4. Let children stick stars around the edges of the card.

5. You may display these or let the children take them home.

★★★

photo

_____
Autograph
_____

NAME: _____ _____ _____

BIRTHDATE: _____ _____ _____

FAVORITE SPORTS TEAM: _____

FAVORITE BOOK: _____

FAVORITE SCHOOL SUBJECT (other than recess) _____

FAVORITE ACTIVITY: _____

BEST FRIENDS: _____

★★★

Patterns

name tag pattern

Who Are They?

The names of the following characters are hidden along the word path. As you find them, circle them.

Max Malone   Little Patty   Amazing Burtoni

Mrs. Filbert   Austin Healy   Mrs. Malone

Gordy   Rosalie Malone   Anthony Baker

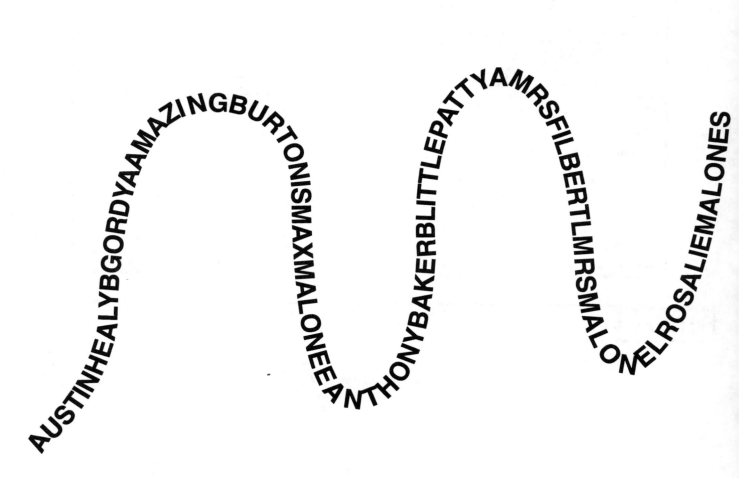

Unscramble and print the leftover letters here.

__ __ __ __ __ __ __ __ __ __

What is important about this word? _____

_____.

You're Invited!

Orp's Birthday Party!

Based on the books by Suzy Kline

Celebrate Orp's 12th Birthday: Program (60–90 minutes)

I've been to Orp's birthday party at:

Story: *Orp* Read this story to the children.

Project: **Book Banners** (Instructions on p. 148)

Story: *Orp Goes to the Hoop* Tell this story to the children.

Game: **Muffin Tin Ball** (Instructions on p. 148)

Story: *Orp and the FBI* Tell this story to the children.

Booktalks: Highlight the other Orp books. Tell about one incident from each, but do not reveal the ending. Encourage the children to read the books on their own.

Activity: **Making Mysteries** (Instructions on p. 148)

Snacks: Light the candles on the cake and sing "Happy Birthday to Orp." Blow out the candles and make a wish. Give each child a piece of cake and a cup of juice.

Story Give children their story bags as they leave.

Bags: Make sure they have their banners and their Mysteries.

Planning and Promotion

Advertising Display: Have a large poster with Orp shooting hoops. Have the program and registration information printed on the poster. Provide flyers with the program information for people to take as reminders.

Room Decorations: Use a basketball theme. Have banners, balloons and streamers. Make a large banner that says HAPPY BIRTHDAY, ORP. Try to find a tablecloth, plates, cups and napkins with a basketball theme.

Name Tags: Look for self-stick name tags with a basketball theme.

Snacks: Have a cake with a basketball theme. Write "Happy Birthday, Orp" across the cake. Insert twelve candles.

Story Bags: Give each child a brown lunch sack with a sign attached that says, **I'VE BEEN TO ORP'S BIRTHDAY PARTY AT** _____ . The children can use these to carry home prizes, the puzzle on p. 149 and a bookmark listing all of the Orp materials owned by your library. Party prizes can include items related to the Orp stories.

Materials and Prep

Orp books by Suzy Kline

Books are listed in series order.

Orp. New York: Putnam, 1989. Orp decides to form an "I Hate My Name Club."

Orp and the Chop Suey Burgers. New York: Putnam, 1990. Orp enters a cooking contest. He hopes to win a trip to Disney World.

Orp Goes to the Hoop. New York: Putnam, 1991. Orp has made the A team. But on the night of the game, he is no where around.

Who's Orp's Girlfriend? New York: Putnam, 1993. Orp is faced with a real problem. He has two girlfriends!

Orp and the FBI. New York: Putnam, 1995. Orp and his friend Derrick start their own detective agency. When Orp's sister starts a rival agency, things become very interesting.

Instructions for Book Banners

Materials
1 metal clothes hanger per child
1 12" x 36" piece of heavy duty white paper per child
crayons and markers
pencils
book tape

Directions
Do this as a group, one step at a time.
1. Give each child a piece of paper.
2. Tell them to design a book banner that will encourage others to read a book. Explain that they need to use pictures and words on their banner. *(You may want to have a list of suggested titles to choose from.)*
3. When the banners are finished, show the children how to fold over the top edge so that it fits over the hanger.
4. Tape the banner across the back seam.
5. Hang these from the ceiling in the hallway or other area where they will be well seen.

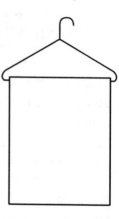

Instructions for Making Mysteries

Materials
1 12" x 18" piece of construction paper per child
1 pencil per child
crayons and markers
glue sticks
notebook paper
newspaper headlines

Directions
1. Give each child a piece of notebook paper and a pencil.
2. Let each child choose a headline.
3. Tell the children to create a mystery that could go with the headline they chose.
   They must create their own, original mysteries. Have them write about what happened. What were the clues? Who solved the mystery? How was it solved?
4. Give each child a piece of construction paper. Tell them to fold it in half to make a booklet.
5. Have the children illustrate their mystery on the front, inside and back. Have them add their names to the front of the booklet.
6. Have children glue their mysteries inside the booklets.
7. If you want, you can read these aloud.

Instructions for Muffin Tin Ball

Materials
3 muffin tins

9 ping pong balls

3 box tops to hold the muffin tins

1 prize per child (*shoelaces, key rings, basketball eraser*)

Directions
1. Have three children come up front.
2. Give each a muffin tin and three ping pong balls.
3. Have them try to get the three balls into the openings within 15 seconds.
4. Award prizes to children as they master this skill. Make sure everyone wins.

Where is Orp?

Here are some people, places and events in the Orp stories. Circle the letters where each joins together. What do the circled letters spell? _____.

Why is this important?

_____.

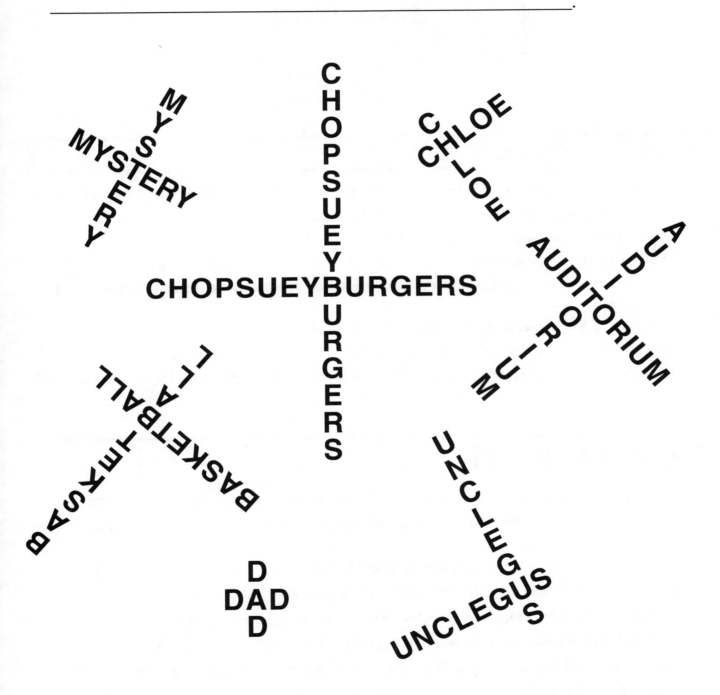

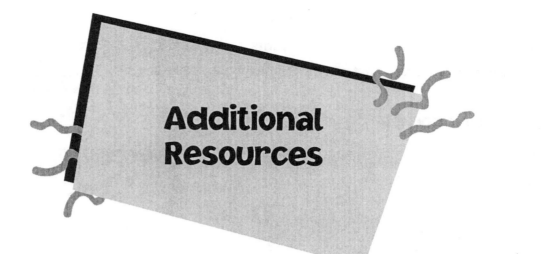

Additional Resources

Storytelling Resources

Bauer, Caroline Feller. *New Handbook for Storytellers.* Chicago: American Library Association, 1993.

————. *Read for the Fun of It.* Bronx: H.W. Wilson, 1992.

————. *This Way to Books.* New York: H.W. Wilson, 1983.

Cooper, Cathie Hilterbran. *The Storyteller's Cornucopia.* Fort Atkinson, WI: Alleyside Press, 1992.

Lima, Carolyn and John. *A to Zoo: Subject Access to Children's Picture Books,.* New York: Bowker, 1993 *(periodically updated).*

Marsh, Valerie. *Storyteller's Sampler.* Fort Atkinson, WI: Alleyside Press, 1996.

Pellowski, Anne. *The Storytelling Handbook.* New York: Simon & Schuster, 1995.

Perry, Phyllis. *Reading Activities and Resources That Work.* Fort Atkinson, WI: Highsmith Press, 1997.

Flannelboard Resources

The books listed here have flannelboard patterns. These patterns can also be used for name tags.

Anderson, Paul S. *Storytelling With the Flannelboard.* Minneapolis, MN: T.S. Denison, 1963-1990 (3 volumes).

Bay, Jeanette Graham. *A Treasury of Flannelboard Stories.* Fort Atkinson, WI: Alleyside, 1995.

Chadwick, Roxane. *Felt Board Story Times* Fort Atkinson, WI: Alleyside, 1997.

Darling, Kathy. *Holiday Hoopla: Flannelboard Fun.* Carthage, IL: Good Apple, 1990.

Sierra, Judy. *The Flannelboard Storytelling Book.* New York: H.W. Wilson Co., 1987.

Taylor, Frances and Gloria G. Vaughn. *The Flannelboard Storybook.* Atlanta, Humanics LTD., 1986.

Warren, Jean. *Mix and Match Series.* Everett, WA: Warren, 1990.

Wilmes, Liz and Dick. *Felt Board Fun.* Elgin, IL: Building Blocks, 1984.

Flannelboard Resources

These companies have beautifully ready made flannelboards and backgrounds.

Lakeshore Learning Materials
2695 Dominquez St.
Carson, CA 90749
800-421-5354

The Storyteller
306 E. 800 South
P.O. Box 921

Resources for Party Prizes, Name Tags and Props

The following companies carry nametag patterns, party prizes and props.
Write or call them to request a catalog.

American Teaching Aids
4424 W. 78th St.
Bloomington, MN. 55435
800-526-9907

Bookmates
One Park Avenue
Old Greenwich, CT. 06870
800-243-4504

Instructional Fair
P.O. Box 1650
Grand Rapids, MI 49501
800-443-2976

Lakeshore Learning Materials
2965 E. Dominguez St.
Carson, CA 90749
800-421-5354

Oriental Trading Company
P.O. Box 2308
Omaha, NE 68103
800-228-2269

Also check teacher stores, party stores and children's bookstores.

Registration

Those of you presenting these programs in public libraries will need to register the children who plan to attend. An index card system works well. Use 4"x 6" cards, and purchase a two-drawer file to accommodate them. These cards come in a wide variety of colors and can be ordered through your paper supplier or local office products store. Divide the cards by session, each session using a different color card. File them alphabetically by the child's last name.

File Waiting List cards in a separate section. Use white cards for the waiting list. If children cancel, you can fill the vacancies from the waiting list. Number the cards and file them in numerical order. The first child on the list will be the first invited if there is a cancellation.

The information requested on the card allows you to gather interesting statistics. You can find out how many children from each school attend, the number of children in each age group or grade and what area of town children are coming from.

It's recommended to have printed copies of registration polices on hand. If people question your policies, you can present your policies verbally and in writing.

Registration Card

> **REGISTRATION CARD**
> (Please print neatly)
>
> PROGRAM NAME: _____
>
> DATE: _____ SESSION/TIME: _____
>
> CHILD'S NAME: _____
> (The way it is to appear on the nametag.)
>
> CHILD'S BIRTHDATE: _____ GRADE: _____
>
> CHILD'S ADDRESS: _____
>
> _____
>
> CHILD'S PHONE: _____ SCHOOL: _____
>
> CHILD'S LIBRARY CARD NO: _____

Registration Card

1. Use 4" x 6" index cards.

2. Use a different colored card for each session.

3. Files cards all the cards for one session together. However, file them alphabetically by last name.

4. Use dividers to separate each session in your file drawer.

5. If a child cancels, write the date of cancellation on the card, and keep it in the back of the file. Note who called in the cancellation.

Waiting List Card

WAITING LIST CARD   **Number** _____
(Please print neatly.)

PROGRAM NAME: _____

DATE: _____ SESSION/TIME: _____

CHILD'S NAME: _____
(The way it is to appear on the nametag.)

CHILD'S BIRTHDATE: _____ GRADE: _____

CHILD'S ADDRESS: _____

_____

CHILD'S PHONE: _____ SCHOOL: _____

CHILD'S LIBRARY CARD NO: _____

1. Use white 4" x 6" index cards.

2. Remember to number them as children register. It also helps to note the time and date on the card, especially when many registrations come in together.

3. Children should be moved from the waiting list in the order that they signed up.

4. File the cards by number rather than alphabetically.

5. When moving a card from the waiting list to a program, you can either fill out a color-coded card or move the white one into the proper program slot. When you use the white card, be sure to note the program session (time and date) the child move to.

Room Arrangement Floor Plans

On the next page are copies of room arrangement floor plans. You will probably have to adapt these according to your needs, but they will provide a starting point.

Try to have an open area where children can sit on the floor and listen to stories and booktalks. Have the work tables set up to the back or sides of the room.

When working with preschool programs that include parents, you can have the parents sit on the floor next to their children. Another option is to seat the children in the first three rows and seat the parents behind the entire group. It's important to make sure that children can see you. Make certain that smaller children sit in front with the taller children behind them, so that the view of shorter people is not blocked.

Be flexible. Some children prefer or need to sit by a parent, while others prefer to sit alone with a parent in the back.

When working at the activity tables, parents can stand or kneel alongside their children. If space permits, you can add chairs for the parents, so they can sit next to their child.

For those of you using a school classroom, try moving the desks, so they are along the sides and back of the room. You can use a table or the tops of low shelving units for the snack table. Let the children sit on the floor in the center of the desks.

If your area is uncarpeted, consider purchasing some colorful bathroom carpet, a carpet remnant, or a braided rug for the children to sit on. It's more comfortable and cozy with a rug. I prefer this to individual carpet squares. Children can't move around as easily, and they tend to trip on the squares. A large rug can be easily taken up and moved when necessary.

This set-up seats 20 children

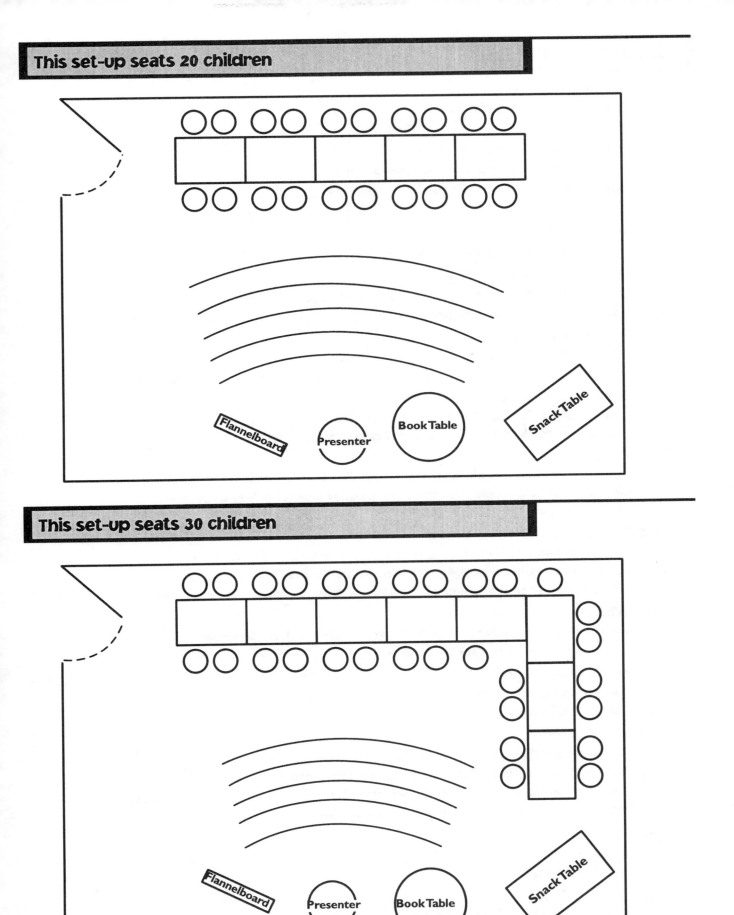

This set-up seats 30 children

P. 64: A Secret Message:
Amelia Bedelia does silly things.

P. 77: Someone Silly
Down: 1. Halloween 2. Norman 3. Lunch 4. Read
Across: 1. Honey 2. Girl 3. Tooth 4. Bikes 5. Valentine

P. 81: What a Mess!
Doug, Song Lee, Sidney, Mary, Ida, Dexter, Miss Mackle, Harry (Kids)

P. 85: Where Are They?
Mary, Elizabeth, Mom, Marvin, Fred, Audrey, Dad (Mrs. Bird, teacher)

P. 109: Something Queer Has Happened
Down: 1. Solve 2. Painting 3. Fletcher 4. Goldfish 5. Murdock 6. Lazy
Across: 1. Tofu 2. Marshall 3. Fingerprint 4. Missing 5. Salami 6. Braces 7. Castle (Elizabeth Levy)

P. 113: Reading Henry's Journal
1. Agony 2. Midge, Research 3. Belinda, Hide 4. Amos 5. Grand Canyon
6. Galileo 7. Rodeo 8. Service 9. Allowances 10. Kite, Contest (Grovers Corners, New Jersey)

P. 117: Something to Solve:
Dinosaurs, Arkansas, Cats, Alabama, Gymnastics, Tennis, Chile, Whales,
Maine, Trains, Scotland, Archery (Amanda Martin, Matthew's sister)

P. 121: Puzzling
Millie Cooper, Miss Brennan, Sandy Feinman, OJ Goodwin, Howard Hall, Natalie
Bloom, Freddy Simon, Elmer Bass, Myra Glass, Lenore Simon, Rochelle Lieberman,
Marlene Kaufman, Letty Loeb, Angela Moretti (Reynolds Rocket)

P. 125: Happy Birthday, Amber Brown
1. Amber Brown Is Not a Crayon, 2. You Can't Eat Your Chicken Pox, Amber Brown,
3. Amber Brown Goes Fourth, 4. Amber Brown Wants Extra Credit,
5. Forever Amber Brown, 6. Amber Brown Sees Red (Amberino, Amber's nickname)

P. 129. Who's This?
1. Raymond 2. Miss Pinkham 3. John 4. Margie 5. Hamburger Head 6. Herbie
7. Olivia 8. Philip 9. Mr. Hodgekiss (Annabelle)

P. 134: Who's Their Friend?
Mary, Grace, Caroline, Miss Wilder, Willie, Carrie, Laura, Indians,
Charles, (Mr. Edwards)

P. 142: Help Wanted
Cam Jansen and the Mystery of the UFO, Stolen Diamonds, Dinosaur Bones,
Monster Movie, Television Dog, Flight 54, Carnival Prize, Babe Ruth Baseball, Chocolate
Fudge, Monkey House, Circus Clown, Triceratops Pops, Gold Coins, Stolen Corn Popper,
Haunted House, Ghostly Mystery (Jennifer Jansen, Cam Jansen)

P. 146: Who Are They?
Baseballs, Max & Gordy bought them cheap and sold them to kids who wanted
to get them autographed.

P. 149: Where Is Orp?
Bathtub. That's where Orp sits and thinks.

Activity Finder Index

	Animals	Art	Booktalks	Creative Writ.	Games	Guest Charact.	Library Skills	Movement	Music	Mysteries	Parent Involve.	Photos	Puppets	Reading Prog.	Rhymes	Social Studies	Treasure Hunt	Section starts on page...
Preschool–Kindergarten																		
Christina Katerina			✔			✔			✔	✔			✔					13
Corduroy Bear	✔		✔			✔			✔	✔			✔	✔				✔	17
Nora			✔			✔			✔	✔			✔					22
Peter			✔			✔			✔	✔			✔					25
Harold			✔						✔	✔			✔				✔	29
Bill Crocodile	✔		✔			✔		✔	✔	✔			✔				✔	33
Louanne Pig	✔		✔			✔			✔	✔			✔	✔				37
Miffy Rabbit	✔		✔			✔			✔	✔			✔	✔				42
Mother Goose	✔		✔			✔	✔		✔	✔		✔	✔	✔				47
Spot	✔		✔			✔			✔	✔			✔	✔		✔	✔	55
Kindergarten–2nd Grade																		
Amelia Bedelia			✔	✔	✔	✔	✔											60
Jimmy	✔		✔	✔		✔								✔	✔			65
Pinkerton	✔		✔	✔	✔	✔			✔	✔								69
Arthur Monkey	✔		✔	✔		✔				✔								74
Horrible Harry			✔	✔		✔			✔									78
Mary Maroney			✔	✔		✔		✔	✔									82
Strega Nona			✔	✔		✔											✔	86
Nate the Great			✔	✔	✔	✔	✔	✔	✔		✔		✔				✔	90
Frances Badger	✔		✔	✔		✔			✔							✔		96
Amanda Pig	✔		✔	✔					✔									101
3rd –5th Grades																		
Gwen			✔	✔								✔						106
Henry Reed			✔	✔	✔		✔									✔		110
Matthew Martin			✔	✔	✔	✔	✔											114
Millie Cooper			✔	✔	✔	✔								✔				118
Amber Brown			✔	✔		✔						✔						122
Herbie Jones			✔	✔	✔	✔		✔	✔									126
Laura Ingalls			✔	✔		✔	✔									✔		130
Cam Jansen			✔	✔	✔			✔			✔						✔	135
Max Malone			✔	✔	✔	✔										✔		143
Orp			✔	✔	✔	✔					✔							147

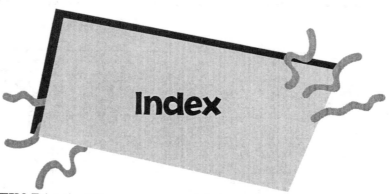

Index

SUBJECTS are listed in CAPITAL LETTERS. Titles of activities, games, songs and rhymes are listed in lower case letters. See p. 157 for an index of activities sorted by activity type.